**W9-CTY-462**

GIVE US THIS DAY OUR DAILY BREAD

*Colleen Townsend Evans*

# GIVE US THIS DAY
# OUR DAILY BREAD

**ASKING FOR AND SHARING LIFE'S NECESSITIES**

A DOUBLEDAY-GALILEE ORIGINAL

DOUBLEDAY & COMPANY, INC.
GARDEN CITY, NEW YORK
1981

Permission to quote from the following sources is gratefully acknowledged:

From *Something Beautiful for God* by Malcolm Muggeridge, copyright ©
1971 by The Mother Teresa Committee. Reprinted by permission of
Harper & Row, Publishers, Inc.

From *George Mueller* by Basil Miller, published and copyright © 1972,
Bethany Fellowship, Inc., Minneapolis, Minnesota 55438.

From *The Collected Poems* of Thomas Merton. Copyright © 1957 by
The Abbey of Gethsemani, Inc. Reprinted by permission of New Directions.

From The New English Bible. Copyright © 1961, 1970 by The Delegates of
The Oxford University Press and the Syndics of the Cambridge University
Press. Reprinted by permission.

Biblical quotations are taken from
the Revised Standard Version
unless otherwise noted.

to

Mary Jane          Mimi
and               and
John              George

who
in obedience to their Lord
have learned well the
ways of sharing

IN  APPRECIATION


with thanks
to
Laura Hobe and Marilee Melvin
for their
friendship and gift
of HELPS

There is plenty for all of us to do. . . . I do think that if people were to see, really *see* when they look, many things could happen. Very often we don't take notice of the people suffering near us. . . . And yet, consider the family I recently gave rice to after I heard they hadn't eaten for a long time. After I gave her the rice, the mother quietly divided the rice into two portions, and left the house. When she returned, I asked her where she had gone. "To my neighbor's," she answered, "with half the rice. Like me, they are also starving."

*Mother Teresa of Calcutta*

# PREFACE

Prayer and our relationship with God are inseparably inter-twined, because it is through prayer that we communicate with God. Clement of Alexandria said, "Prayer is conversation with God"—and this is true. Sometimes we may not even use words, but may simply experience an outpouring of our deepest feelings. For Thomas Merton, prayer was "a consciousness of one's union with God, an awareness of one's inner self."

Prayer is mysterious. As Edwin Keith described it, "Prayer is exhaling the spirit of man and inhaling the spirit of God." The current runs both ways—from man to God and God to man—and there is no area of our lives it cannot touch. It truly is a "rising up and a drawing near to God in mind, and in heart, and in spirit" (Alexander Whyte). It is the way we bring all that we are, and all of our world, into contact with all that is God.

But—this is not a book on the broad subject of prayer. Tempting as it is to contemplate general principles, I realize that many excellent books have already been written, and by men and women whose authority is far greater than mine. And so, in this book, I want only to share with you some of my thoughts and convictions on one aspect of prayer—the kind we call petitionary prayer. This is the way we ask God for our daily needs, and it was Jesus himself who told us to ask when he taught us the words "Give us this day our daily bread."

This book, then, is about praying for life resources, but not in an "I-me-my" sense. When we ask for "our daily bread," it means we ask not only for ourselves, but also for others. And when the resources come, they are not only for us. They are meant to be shared.

# CONTENTS

## PART IV—THE IMPERATIVE TO SHARE

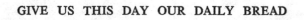

GIVE US THIS DAY OUR DAILY BREAD

# PART I

## BEFORE WE ASK

**Chapter 1**

# Tell Me About Your God

There is only one God, but there are many misconceptions about him—and when we mistake the false for the true, the results can be tragic. We become like the woman who protested to a minister friend of ours, "I don't believe in God! How can you believe in someone who's always waiting to punish us for the slightest wrong we do, someone who enjoys seeing us suffer? No, I'm sorry, I can't believe in such a God!"

Our friend, who is very kind and perceptive, said simply, "Tell me more about this god. I don't think I believe in him, either."

I know many people who believe—but in the wrong kind of god. Ellen was one of them. She was a sweet-faced woman in her early sixties when I came to know her a few years ago, but she seemed troubled. She had been brought up in a legalistic home, and probably her parents had been brought up in the same way. Surely they were well intentioned. But Ellen's god, as presented to her by her parents, was a stern, insensitive, unmerciful judge who seemed to be interested only in punishing Ellen whenever she disobeyed her parents. Actually, Ellen was a good child, but more out of fear of God's anger than any joy in goodness itself. No matter what misfortune entered her life, she felt she had only herself to blame. She never considered asking her god for help or comfort. In fact, the less she had to do with him, the better. When she left home and went away to college, she happily felt free of him at last. She married, and for thirty years she never went to church.

But deep inside, she had the uneasy feeling that eventually there would be some kind of punishment waiting for her. Not quite understanding why, she started attending the church my husband serves. Then she joined the Women's Association and a Bible study class on the nature of the Christian faith. We could see the surprise growing on her face as she associated with people who believed in a different God. She was astonished by the radiance in their lives, by their eagerness to be close to their Lord, and by the ease with which they brought their burdens to him, knowing they would be understood and comforted.

How could this be? Ellen wondered. Can their God and my god be the same person? One day she called the woman who was heading our new church counseling center, an understanding woman with professional training. It was only after a number of conversations, in which Ellen poured out her bitter and confused feelings about the god of her childhood, that she really began to accept a God of love.

Ellen was like a flower opening to the sun, and it was beautiful to watch her faith bloom. Having a different God made her a different person—outgoing, trusting, confident of the future. And then, a few months ago, she went to her doctor for a routine checkup—which revealed a tumor in the abdomen.

When I heard the news, I was concerned. Ellen's trust in a loving God was young—very possibly still fragile—and I wondered how she would cope with a situation that would be a struggle for any of us. How would she face the fear of the unknown?

I called her and she was buoyant. "If this had happened to me a few years ago," she told me, "I would have been a basket case. I would have been certain I was being punished for not going to church all these years. But now I know who God really is, and I can go to him for help. I can ask him to take away my fear. I can ask him to heal me—because he's my Father, and he loves me!"

Ellen went into the hospital for exploratory surgery, and the tumor was malignant. There was further surgery, and now there is chemotherapy. And through it all, Ellen has been an inspiration to everyone who knows her. Her trust in God's ability to heal her has been amazing. "But if it's not my time to be healed," she told me, "I'm ready for that, too. All I know is that I am a woman at peace."

If only everyone who believes in the wrong kind of god could find the real One. If only everyone who lives in terror of spiritual abandonment could experience Ellen's new security. Lives would be changed, because our concept of God shapes our thoughts and feelings. In fact, the kind of God we believe in shapes our very lives and determines the kind of people we become. It also determines the way we pray.

Back in the sixties, the "death of God" theologians were writing disparagingly about prayer, which isn't so hard to understand. For if we don't feel, bone-deep in our beings, that our God is Someone who loves and cares about us in a real, personal way, then why ask him for anything?—ever? And if our concept of God is a fuzzy I-know-you're-out-there-*some*where kind of spiritual influence, then that's the way we pray. After all, how *do* you communicate with a "principle of concretion" or an "integrating factor in experience"? How *do* you pray to a "Life Essence"? How can you possibly have any kind of a relationship with an abstract maven?

And yet the Christian view of God is that he is good, loving, personal, and very real. Our God invites us to have a relationship with him and to pray. "At all times, pray," Jesus said, "and do not lose heart" (Luke 18:1).

The real God is unmistakably recognizable by his love. For not only does he love, but love is his very essence. Out of love, he created the world. Out of love, he created humankind. Out of love, he is deeply involved in our daily lives, and he wants us to have whatever we need to develop the abilities he gave us. He wants to "resource" us for life and service, because he has a place for all of us, no matter who or where we are, and a task for each of us to do. That's what we mean by "unconditional love"—no strings attached. It's a love that never ends—even if we turn away, God is always there.

I know what that love is because some years ago, before I voluntarily became part of the Christian family, I saw it reflected in the lives of my Christian friends, and knew I would never feel whole until I experienced it, too. Until that time I considered myself a Christian because I believed in God. But I didn't *know* him in a personal way—I didn't even realize such a relationship was possible. Still, I could see that my friends knew God in a totally different way than I did. Their relationship with him was so close, while mine was distant. God was their friend, Someone with whom they could discuss *anything*, while to me, God was—well, *God*.

I also noticed an exquisite joy in my friends that had nothing to do with their earthly circumstances. No matter what happened to them, this joy persisted, because, as I learned later, they knew they were loved—and love shows on people. It gave them an identity, an unwavering security, and a sense of purpose I longed to discover. They were less concerned about themselves than I was, and more sensitive to the feelings and needs of others—in fact, that was how they drew me into their circle, for which I will be forever grateful.

And then, one day, that love invaded my life as I consciously yielded my will to Jesus Christ, and I began to understand why my friends couldn't give me what they had. Only God could, and he most graciously gave generously to me. Nothing has been the same for me since that moment.

But—tell me about *your* God. Do you feel *loved* by him—exactly the way you are, with all your strengths and weaknesses? Do you feel *forgiven*—welcomed into his family —convinced of his goodness and care for you in every part of your life?

If your answer is yes, then you have the strong foundation you need for your prayers. You believe in the good and loving God who is our Father—and you know he is even much more eager to give than we are to ask.

## Chapter 2

## *Teach Me to Pray*

"Pray for me," a friend asks during a time of deep sorrow.

"Pray with me," whispers a woman in a hospital waiting room as she bows her head and reaches for a neighbor's hand.

"Let us pray," the minister says, leading his congregation in a prayer that is sometimes formal and spoken, sometimes silent.

"Daddy, come and say prayers with me?" asks a sleepy child kneeling by her bed.

"I'll have to pray about this," says a man facing an important decision.

"Wow! Thank you, Lord!" a young hiker exclaims as he makes his way over the ridge of a mountain that opens up an outrageously beautiful view of the valley below.

And a man, sitting alone in his room, clasps his hands, lifts his tear-streaked face, and communes with God through sighs too deep for words.

There are many kinds of prayers, and many ways to speak them—and yet there is no single way that is right . . . or correct . . . or proper. Nor is there a wrong way to pray. One either prays, or one does not.

Yes, but, you say, there *must* be some rules one can follow if one wants to learn how to pray. Everything has a *how*— *How* should we pray?

At one time or another, most of us have pondered this question. Do we simply open our lips and talk to God? Or should we use special words, perhaps words more lofty than we ordinarily use when conversing with a friend? Can we talk about anything under the sun? Or are there only certain matters we should mention to a divine Creator?

Should we pray out loud? Or silently? With head bowed? Or lifted upward? Or facing straight ahead? Must we close our eyes? Or can we leave them open? Is it better to pray alone? Or with someone? In the morning and at night? At mealtimes? In church? Anytime? Anywhere?

There is no *one* way to pray, and we know that from the example of Jesus himself. Prayer was the natural atmosphere of his daily life, the breath of his soul, as we learn from almost every page of the gospels, where it is recorded that "Jesus prayed." In Mark 1:35, "a great while before day," Jesus got up and prayed. In Mark 6:46, after feeding the five thousand their noonday meal, he took "leave of them" and "went into the hills to pray." In Mark 7:34, we read that when crowds pressed around him, clamoring for his help, he sent his "thought prayers" heavenward, asking for and receiving the strength he needed.

In Luke 3:21–22, Jesus prayed about his vocation: "Jesus also being baptized, and praying, the heaven was opened, and the Holy Spirit descended" (KJV). In Luke 6:12, he asked for God's guidance in choosing his disciples: "He went out into a mountain to pray, and continued all night in prayer to God" (KJV).

He did not hesitate to ask his Father to help him in his ministry. For instance, when the demoniac came rushing to him, begging for release from his madness, Jesus said, "This kind [of demon] can come forth by nothing, but by prayer" (Mark 9:29; KJV).

In Gethsemane, when he was tempted to turn his back on

God's way for him, Luke tells us that "being in an agony he prayed" (22:44) and was enabled to resist. And finally, in dying, Jesus prayed: "Father, forgive them . . ." (Luke 23:34), and " . . . Into thy hands I commend my spirit" (Luke 23:46; KJV).

Surely there were also times of private prayer, when no one was about to record them.

The disciples, living in close relationship to Jesus, must have noticed the many different ways and times he prayed. They also must have become aware of the difference between his prayers and theirs. Yes, they prayed, but their prayers failed to achieve the close relationship with God that Jesus knew. How they must have yearned for such an experience! We can almost hear them murmuring among themselves as they watched from a short distance while Jesus "was praying in a certain place" (Luke 11:1). And, witnessing the depth of the communion he had with his Father, they could hold back no longer. " . . . when he ceased, one of his disciples said to him, Lord, teach us to pray" (Luke 11:1). Like so many of us, they wanted to learn the *right* way to pray.

But Jesus didn't give them a how-to course in prayer. He didn't offer them a list of do's and don'ts. He didn't even lecture to them about prayer. He taught them how to pray by praying with them and by the way he lived. Praying was an integral part of his life.

Jesus prayed in many different places—in the quiet, lonely wilderness . . . along the highways and roads . . . in homes . . . in the temple . . . in the midst of a crowd and during the busiest moments of his life. He prayed in many different ways—alone, with friends, with strangers; with his eyes closed and also with them open; kneeling, standing, walking.

In the words of Dr. James S. Stewart of Scotland: "What Christ would have us realize is that God is alive and God is free, and that therefore true faith will always do as Jesus himself did and carry its requests straight to the throne."

The right way to pray, then, is any way that allows us to communicate with God. For prayer is not a ritual; it is the soul's inherent response to a relationship with a loving Father.

I remember that when I was a new Christian, I felt very much as the disciples must have felt when they watched Jesus praying. I had prayed all my life, and yet I was missing something that my Christian friends seemed to be getting through their prayers. I couldn't quite define it, but I knew it was vitally important. I kept wishing one of them would draw me aside and say, "Now, Colleen, this is how you should pray . . ." and then go on to demonstrate, step by step. But that never happened.

Instead, one day a friend sidled up to me and said, "A group of us meet every Saturday morning at 6 A.M. . . . Come pray with us!" Not "This is how you pray"—just "Come pray with us!" I swallowed hard, said I would, and set my alarm for a very early hour.

The group comprised mostly young college students, members of the Hollywood Presbyterian Church—which was experiencing a tremendous spiritual renewal at that time—and, with the exception of me, they were leaders in the congregation. They met to pray in the home of Dr. Henrietta Mears, the church's director of Christian Education, a remarkable and inspiring woman of God, who believed that one should pray boldly, and taught us how simply by doing it.

I had never been in such a group. We assembled in Dr. Mears's dining room, where chairs had been set up around the table for us. We came in silently, not even greeting each other, for in that early dawn stillness there was a special importance to the attitude of prayer. Each of us knelt down by a chair and prayed—silently—until someone, in a very natural way, began to pray out loud. It didn't matter who began or who spoke next, for there was a very real sense of the Spirit being in control.

I had never heard such prayers! We prayed for a greater spiritual awakening among ourselves and asked God to develop in us a sense of faithfulness and accountability to him and to others. We prayed for friends, for family, for those in pain and suffering, asking God to bless their lives. We prayed for the work of the Lord in all parts of the world, in all events, and in the hearts of all people. Like Dr. Mears, our teacher, we "prayed big."

For a long time I prayed silently, almost trembling at the thought of praying out loud. But no one said I had to—and even though I was silent, my heart and mind were deeply involved in the prayers I heard.

And the words I heard—simple, ordinary words, the kind one would use speaking to a dear friend or person one loved, which is exactly what our heavenly Father is. Everyone prayed in a natural, spontaneous way, some eloquently, some falteringly—no matter, God understood the feelings underneath the words.

Then, one Saturday morning, as we knelt around the now familiar table, I was especially moved and I heard my own voice speaking out loud. No one was more surprised than I! Praying out loud was something that just happened, something that simply came out of the love, warmth, and friendship I was feeling with Jesus Christ. And through my prayers, my acquaintance with him was deepening.

I feel I'd like to explain something here. Before I made a commitment to Christ I had a vague belief in God, and the prayers I prayed were genuine and sincere. And I believe God heard me when I prayed. But my prayers then were very limited in their scope: they were mainly me-centered and more like wishes than anything else, because at that time my spiritual life was practically an embryo. But as I began to pray out of a new and focused relationship with God—as prayer became my communication with my heavenly Father—praying took on much greater dimensions. It grew in every possible direction. My soul was breathing! I was entering areas I had never dreamed of before—and I was no longer earthbound! This growth through prayer continues even now.

So although this little book is addressed to prayers of petition, make no mistake: prayer is *much* more than asking. Prayer is taking *all* of life to God, and we can do that anywhere we are, at any time, using whichever words come to our minds—or no words at all.

There is no one place where we should pray. Rather, there are many, depending upon the moment, the need, and the circumstances.

I like to begin my day with prayer, but, as I am not a bright-eyed morning person, it is often a simple, sleepy prayer committing the day to God.

On my bedside table I keep a list of people I want to pray for—and although I resisted using a list for a long time, I finally had to acknowledge that I was quite capable of forgetting a name or two if I didn't write them all down. Praying for specific persons in the morning keeps their needs before me throughout the day, and when I find other moments here and there, I pray for those needs again.

I often pray "on the run," because it is easy and convenient and fits into a busy, sometimes hectic schedule. I pray as I work, even as I drive, and usually silently—I call these my "thought prayers."

I like the way my husband, Louie, gets additional prayer time out of city traffic when he is driving: instead of fuming at red lights and snarled intersections, he uses these chinks of time to remember those with whom he has made a covenant of prayer.

In many ways, thought prayers are like talking to one's self —with the very important difference that one is talking to God instead. This is one of the ways we can praise God for the beauty we see around us. We can also seek his guidance for the work we are doing, and ask for his help in making decisions. We can send off a spontaneous prayer for someone we see—and don't know—who looks lonely or troubled.

At night, before going to sleep—and through my "prayers

on the run"—I also commit the day's events to God and ask him to use them for his glory. If there have been problems or difficulties, I ask him to take their burdens from me—and I ask to abide with him while I sleep, because, as Brother Lawrence said, "the barque of the soul goeth forward even in sleep."

I am grateful for prayers on the run, especially because they allow me to talk to the Lord all day long—"prayer without ceasing"—and still do his work in a practical sense. But praying is more than being heard by God—and more than hearing when he speaks. Because it is a relationship with someone we love, and because we want that relationship to deepen, prayer does require time alone, without distractions, and even without the good company of others we love. It requires us to spend some time absolutely alone with God, as Jesus specified when he said, ". . . go into your room and shut the door and pray to your Father who is in secret" (Matt. 6:6).

But suppose we don't have such a room all to ourselves? Must we spend our lives never knowing what it is to be alone with God?

Since Jesus was well aware that many of those who heard him speak these words would never have a room of their own, perhaps the key to his meaning here is the inner room of our heart. Quite possibly Jesus meant not a physical room with four walls and a door we can lock but, rather, a place within ourselves, a quiet portion of our consciousness reserved for God alone. Everyone, rich and poor alike, has access to such a chamber, where he or she can commune with our Father about the most intimate feelings.

It is also in our inner heart that we can experience the special kind of stillness that enables us to hear God speaking to us. For silence is an important part of prayer; it allows God to bring ideas into our minds, awaken concerns within us, and help us untangle the threads of our daily lives. As his Holy Spirit moves our souls, we can then respond with our actions.

But many of us may feel as Blaise Pascal did when he

wrote: "The eternal silence of these infinite spaces terrifies me." We run from silence because it is here that we come face to face with ourselves—and with God.

Thomas Merton, the Trappist monk who took a vow of silence as a way of life, wrote: "Just remaining quietly in the presence of God, being attentive to Him, requires a lot of courage and know-how." And if we can dare to experience them, we will find these quiet times alone with God not fearful but, rather, a source of deep inner security. "Be still, and know that I am God," he has told us.

Dr. Wayne Oates wrote in *Nurturing Silence in a Noisy Heart:* "As you cease the need to scream, shout, and demand, the very peace and quiet you experience blends into the stillness of God's presence.

"Then watch out! You will think thoughts that you have not thought before. The silence you cultivate becomes the medium of fresh wisdom from the Creator."

Silence need not be awkward or embarrassing, for to be with one you love, without the need for words, is a beautiful and satisfying form of communication.

I remember times when our children were small and used to come running to me, all of them chattering at once about the events of their day—and it was wonderful to hear them and to have them share their feelings with me. But there were also the times when they came to me wanting only to be held, quietly, to be close, to have me stroke their heads and caress them into sleep. And so it is, sometimes, with us and with God our Father.

We, too, become weary of ourselves . . . of others . . . and we come to God without words, needing to be close to him, wanting only to lay our head and our heart on his shoulder . . . and find rest. I think Thomas Merton expressed that need with great sensitivity in his poem:

> Be still
> Listen to the Stones of the Wall

Be silent, they try
To speak your

Name.
Listen
To the living walls.
Who are you?
Who

Are You? Whose
Silence are you?

Who (be quiet)
Are You (as these stones
Are quiet). . . .

The one place in all the world where I most love to be
alone with God is in the high Sierra—where we like to vaca-
tion as a family—but if I were to wait for those times, I would
pray in that way about once a year, and perhaps not that
often. And I need those times alone with God on a daily basis
—so I must find a place for quiet close at hand.

In our house something is almost always going on—
children come and go, friends drop in, members of the congregation come to discuss and share. Even when we have
lived in a house with many rooms, it hasn't always been possible for me to find a space where I can be quiet and alone. So I
have had to improvise—and a place I have found that pleases
me is the old rocking chair in my bedroom.

I have a special fondness for that chair. Louie bought it for
me when we took our first church after seminary and I was
expecting our third baby. It was my nursing chair, and long
after our children grew beyond that need, I loved to sit in my
chair whenever I had the need to nurture the silence in my
heart. This old rocker is my inner chamber when no other
place is available—it doesn't matter what else is going on in
our house, or how many voices interrupt the stillness. As I sit
and rock, the silence I require steals over me, and my chair

serves as my inner chamber. Even if people are in and out of
the room, I can close my eyes and seek the stillness of Christ
in my heart. No matter where we are, he is always near us.

Someone asked recently: Can we pray with our eyes open?

Of course we can—although when I first did it in situations other than driving a car, I wasn't immediately comfortable. I am now, but it took time.

Many of us have thought all along that we had to close our
eyes in order to pray. Juan Carlos Ortiz, in his book *The Disciple,* described his surprise when he realized that this was not
necessary. He was on a retreat in the country with some of his
parishioners and, looking about him at the flowers, the birds,
and the trees, he was moved to praise God for the beauties of
his universe. But he was reluctant to shut out the view as he
prayed. "Lord," he said, "where in the Bible does it say we
must close our eyes to pray?"

"I did a quick dash in my mind from Genesis to Revelation
—I didn't find any such rule. It's not there. In fact, the Bible
shows the opposite; Psalm 121 says, 'I will lift up my eyes to
the mountains.' Jesus began his last prayer by 'lifting up His
eyes to heaven.'"

After that realization, Reverend Ortiz and his congregation
began practicing "eyes-open" prayer, not only when they were
in the country, but also when they met together to pray in
church. They found that this simple method of talking with
God changed the quality of their prayers and worship in that
their prayers became more real, less otherworldly, and seemed
more a natural part of their everyday life. They even stopped
"changing their voice and vocabulary for prayer," and became "less dramatic and flowery."

"With our eyes open," Reverend Ortiz wrote, "we realize
that we must live only one kind of life twenty-four hours a
day. Everything must be done in God's presence; He is always
here. We don't have to put on any special speech for Him."

In recent years, Louie and I have prayed more often with
our eyes open. For us it has become natural and warm to look

at the face of the person about whom—or with whom—we are praying.

Still, there are times when I feel the need to close my eyes while praying, if only to shut out distractions. And sometimes, in the dimness of the inner chamber that closed eyes provide, I have a deeper sense of the Lord's presence. But I welcome the freedom and spontaneity of choosing how I shall pray.

I also welcome being able to talk to God as I would to my most trusted friend—which he is. People don't speak in a stilted manner today, and when we try to use the language of another age and time we are putting an obstacle between ourselves and God.

Not that formal prayers are ineffective. When spoken sincerely, they are powerful instruments, and there are times when nothing speaks for me more profoundly than the prayers found in the Book of Common Worship. And the prayers of John Baillie, in his *Diary of Private Prayer*, are among the most moving and evocative I have ever known.

But, of course, the essence of prayer is not the words or the times or the places we choose, but the attitude of our hearts. For this is what God hears . . . he hears beyond our words to what we truly feel and mean.

There are times when we will be eloquent, or when we will stumble over our own words; and there are times when we will try to pray and be unable to speak a word at all. When we mourn, perhaps, or when we are sorely wounded in spirit, we may desperately need to come to God in prayer, yet the words elude us. Perhaps all we can offer up is a sigh . . . or a single word—"God!" "Lord!" "Help!"—or a tear that streams silently down our face.

Paul spoke of such times when he wrote: "for we do not know how to pray as we ought; but the Spirit himself intercedes for us with sighs too deep for words" (Romans 8:26). This passage means so much to me because I have known times when I have come to God too choked with pain to know what to say—yet needing to make contact with him. And at those times I have remembered Paul's words, and I have asked the Holy Spirit to pray *for* me: "Lord, I can't—*you* pray!" He has never failed me.

I have also known times when I needed to pray with another person, or even with a group. Jesus taught us the importance of this kind of prayer when he said, "where two or three are gathered in my name, there am I in the midst of them" (Matt. 18:20). If prayer is the natural breath of the soul, if it is our spontaneous response to God's loving presence, then we will sense which are the times to pray alone and which are the times when we need the prayers of others.

There is, then, no *one* way to pray, for prayer is an attitude of heart that God perceives whether it comes in the form of a quiet thought, a sigh too deep for words, or spoken aloud. Like the loving conversation between two friends, it should not be restricted by rules and regulations.

Prayer is a free, vital fellowship between the person and the Creator . . . it is life touching Life . . . the gratitude of our hearts finding a voice of praise. And just as we find great joy when our children share their lives and feelings with us, God —our Father—is delighted when we share our lives with him.

There is nothing we cannot say to God. He wants to know about all things, great and small, in our daily living. We can tell him about our sorrows—but also about the things that give us joy. We can ask him to take the burden of anxiety from our hearts as we wrestle with the problems of life. We can ask him for guidance in our relationships with others. We can laugh with him, cry with him, even sigh with him—and he will understand.

God waits for us to come to him in prayer. And because he loves us, nothing about us is unimportant or inconsequential. If it concerns us, it concerns him—that is what makes the relationship of love so very rich.

# Chapter 3

## When We Know the Shepherd

In my mother's Bible, which now belongs to me, I found these
words written in the margin alongside the Twenty-third
Psalm: "He knew the Shepherd." At first I wasn't sure what
she meant by that, but I am beginning to understand.

The writer of the Twenty-third Psalm was the son of a poor
man. He became a hero of his nation and later a mighty king,
because he learned to trust in the Lord to supply all his needs
—spiritual, material, emotional, and physical. To know the
Shepherd is to understand that God is big enough to provide
all our needs—not only the major ones, but the everyday, practical resources we need to live the Christian life. It means that
God can handle anything that happens to us.

"I shall not want" means that we have *nothing* to fear or to
dread. We will lack nothing that is essential when we have the
Shepherd. We are not promised immunity from pain and sorrow in this world, but the Shepherd will provide the inner resource of strength to meet any tribulation. We will never be
left without comfort in difficulty. We will never be denied any
life resource we truly need to grow into the people God wants
us to become.

"I shall not want" means that God is willing and able to
meet our real needs. We are blessed not only by the resources
he gives us, but also by his presence, and we need both. Die-

trich Bonhoeffer, in his little book *Psalms: The Prayer Book of the Bible,* writes: ". . . we need not have a bad conscience when we pray with the Psalter for life, health, peace, and earthly goods if we only recognize, as do the Psalms themselves, that all of this is evidence of the gracious fellowship of God with us, and thereby hold fast to the fact that God's gifts are better than life (Ps. 63:3, f. and Ps. 73:25, f.)."

Asking prayer can take place only when you and I have a relationship with God as our heavenly Father. Then we can ask for our daily bread, as Jesus taught us. Martin Luther said our daily bread "includes everything needed for this life, such as food and clothing, home and property, work and income, a devoted family, an orderly community, good government, favorable weather, peace and health, a good name, and true friends and neighbors." It is also—and most important—the presence of the Giver himself.

We are promised, and can ask for and receive, resources to live abundantly in our spiritual, material, emotional, and physical natures. Ephesians 1:3 tells us that God "has bestowed on us in Christ every spiritual blessing in the heavenly realms" (NEB), and the chapter continues with some extraordinary descriptions of those spiritual blessings. Read it, and remember what resources you have!

Jesus told us that our material needs were on his heavenly Father's mind when he told us, in Matthew 6:25–34, to "put away anxious thoughts about food and drink to keep you alive, and clothes to cover your body. Surely life is more than food, the body more than clothes. Look at the birds of the air; they do not sow and reap and store in barns, yet your heavenly Father feeds them. You are worth more than the birds! . . . do not ask anxiously, 'What are we to eat? What are we to drink? What shall we wear?' . . . your heavenly Father knows that you need them all. Set your mind on God's kingdom and his justice before everything else, and all the rest will come to you as well . . ." (NEB).

On nearly every page of the Bible we see how God supplies

the constant, loving provision of his people's emotional resources. Psalm 103 is an example of the wonderful provision for the waiting heart: "Bless the Lord, my soul; my innermost heart, bless his holy name. Bless the Lord, my soul, and forget none of his benefits. He pardons all my guilt and heals all my suffering. He rescues me from the pit of death and surrounds me with constant love, with tender affection; he contents me with all good in the prime of life, and my youth is ever new like an eagle's" (1–5, NEB).

And for our physical resources, God is also a provider, a heavenly Father, a tender Shepherd. In our physical life we come upon a mystery, for "he was pierced for our transgressions, tortured for our iniquities; the chastisement he bore is health for us and by his scourging we are healed" (Isa. 53:5; NEB)—yet "the grace of God has dawned upon the world with healing for all mankind" (Titus 2:11; NEB). No, they are not contradictory. Sometimes God grants healing to a sick body, sometimes he accomplishes his work not through restoring health but through preparing a spirit to meet him.

In asking for all of our life's resources, which is our right as children of the Father, our attitude is one of grateful praise. For God is infinitely concerned about the life he has given each one of us, and will give us what he knows is best for us to live, serve, and share. As that great Scottish writer of stories George Macdonald once commented, "Man finds it hard to get what he wants, because he does not want the best; God finds it hard to give, because He would give the best, and man will not take it."

## Chapter 4

## *Our Need to Ask*

As children of a loving Father, we have the right to ask God for our daily needs. Not only is this a right he has given us as a sign of his fatherly love, but it is a need we have for ourselves and for the nurturing of our relationship with God.

For my husband and me, one of the great joys of parenthood has been giving our four children the basic things they have needed for life. Of course, they do not have to ask for everything they need. Love, food, shelter, care, support—these, and more, we provide without question. But there are other things we do not give until our children ask for them specifically, and perhaps more than once. Repeated asking over a period of time proves, in their minds and in ours, that their request is not a passing fancy but a deep, lasting desire of the heart.

Our son Tim has wanted to be involved in medicine ever since he was a little boy. As soon as he could read, he devoured books about medicine and those who practice it. My husband and I realized that as children grow up and decide what they want to be, they go through stages. First they may want to be a firefighter, then a doctor, then something else; but not Tim. Medicine was his first and only vocational desire. So when Tim left for college, he knew exactly what he wanted to study, and he was ready to commit himself to the many years of training.

As with all of us, Tim's goal was something he needed help to attain. He has always worked part-time to help pay his expenses, and he has received other forms of aid along the way, but not enough to cover all his costs over such a long time. So, when Tim needs help, we want him to come to us. And he does, he asks—not in a demanding way, as if he were entitled to anything he wanted, but as a son who knows his parents love him and are interested in his future. In fact, as his desires persist, both he and we are convinced of the importance of this goal in his life. Now, just beginning his graduate studies, Tim pursues the dream. And Louie and I are committed to help him reach his goal in any way we can, for it is a goal consistent with his lifelong direction.

As Christians, we have a similar relationship with God, our Father. Of course, God knows what we need—each of us, individually and particularly—and he could easily give it to us without our even asking. But when we ask for something, we usually are quite certain that we need it, and perhaps we would not arrive at that awareness if we simply received all that we needed, automatically. Persistence in prayer helps us to see . . . understand . . . accept. It purifies our desires, so that our very asking becomes more a pilgrimage of discovery than a bothersome tugging at a Father's sleeve. And as we ask, we find ourselves dealing with such basic questions as "Who am I?" and "Lord, what do you want me to do?" Asking enables us to clarify our intentions in life, so that when we receive what we need, we know what to do with it.

Yet there is that question you and I have heard before—many times: "If God loves us so much, and if he knows our needs before we do, why do we have to ask him for anything? Why doesn't he just give it to us?"

Many people—among them, many Christians—believe that petitionary prayer is selfish, and they frown upon it. "God is too great, too busy, to be involved with my little concerns," they say. Or if they don't admit it openly, they secretly believe it in their hearts, which keeps them from practicing and enjoying their full right as a child of God.

The philosopher Immanuel Kant wrote: "It is at once an absurd and presumptuous delusion to try by the insistent importunity of prayer, whether God might not be deflected from the plan of his wisdom to provide some momentary advantage for us." But it was Jesus who said, "Ask, and you will receive; seek, and you will find; knock, and the door will be opened to you" (Matt. 7:7; Good News for Modern Man). He told us to ask our Father for our daily bread—and what could be more basic than that?

Prayer is the little child stretching its arms up to its Father and pleading, "Up, Daddy! Up!" And repeated prayer is simply adding "Please?" It is precisely because God is our Father —a loving Father who desires to give good things to his children—that he tells us to ask of him. Jesus exclaimed, "Is there a father among you who will offer his son a snake when he asks for fish, or a scorpion when he asks for an egg? If you, then, bad as you are, know how to give your children what is good for them, how much more will the heavenly Father give the Holy Spirit [or a good gift] to those who ask him!" (Luke 11:11–13; NEB).

In his book *Unspoken Sermons*, George Macdonald wrote: "Hunger many drive the runaway child home, and he may or may not be fed at once, but he needs his mother more than his dinner. Communion with God is the one need of the soul beyond all other need: prayer is the beginning of that communion, and some need is the motive of that prayer. . . . So begins a communion, a talking with God, a coming-to-one with Him which is the sole end of prayer, yes, of existence itself. . . ."

We never have to make an appointment to talk to God— and we don't have to go "through channels." We have immediate access to the Creator of the Universe through our special relationship to him. When you and I became children of

God, by accepting the gift of life he offers through his Son, we were given family rights and responsibilities. We have the right to ask God to supply our needs as we seek his kingdom and his justice . . . and we have the responsibility to love him and obey his commands.

But first—who is this Person with whom we are now in relationship? and who has given us the right to ask for the basic resources we need to live from day to day as his children?

". . . through him all things came to be; no single thing was created without him. All that came to be was alive with his life, and that life was the light of men" (John 1:3–4; NEB). He is the Source of all creation. He is the loving Creator of our very lives, and of all aspects of our beings—physical, emotional, spiritual, and intellectual. He cares for each of us, personally and individually, and knows us by name: "God loved the world so much that he gave his only Son, that everyone who has faith in him may not die but have eternal life" (John 3:16; NEB). He is our Shepherd, in his tender care for each of us; he is our Rock, protecting us from the heat of the day and the terror of the night; he is our hiding place from the storms of life—not by snatching us away from the storm, but by giving us the means to withstand the buffeting (Isa. 40:11 and John 10:11; 2 Sam. 22:2 and Ps. 71:3; Ps. 119:114). He has our best interests at heart, and delivers us from evil (see Ps. 40:1–3). He gives generously to all of us without making us feel foolish or guilty when we ask for help (James 1:5). He does not help only the "just" (those who are righteous in Christ), but the "unjust" (Matt. 5:45), and he is not willing that *any* person should miss the gift of eternal life in Jesus Christ (Matt. 18:14).

Furthermore, he has revealed himself in his Son, who told us *how* to ask for our daily resources. With his own life, and in his own words, Jesus gave us the key to asking and to relationship with his—and our—Father (Matt. 7:7, Mark 11:24, Luke 11:9–10). He told us to ask, seek, and knock, and to persist in our search with an attitude of grateful faith in a loving Father's goodness. And even Jesus asked his Father on our behalf for the granting of life's resources: "If you love me, you will obey my commands; and I will ask the Father, and he will give you another to be your Advocate, who will be with you for ever—the Spirit of truth" (John 14:16; NEB).

Even now Jesus continues, through the Spirit of truth, to seek us and find us, to help us mature through a relationship of rights and responsibilities with him. "Here I stand knocking at the door; if anyone hears my voice and opens the door, I will come in and sit down to supper with him and he with me" (Rev. 3:20; NEB).

All of prayer is a relationship with God, and asking prayer is a special part of that relationship. Often it is the first step in our relationship with God. For we are needy creatures, and often our needs reach crisis proportions. To whom, then, do we turn? As we tell God about our needs, and listen to him answer us—either by providing for our need, or by using our need and openness to reveal something he wants us to see— our relationship with him grows.

It is interesting to me that the words "ask, seek, knock" in Luke 11 are (in the original Greek) all in the present imperative, the tense of continuing action, so that the meaning is "continually ask," or "Keep on seeking and knocking" (The Interpreter's Bible). It is not only acceptable to God that we ask; he *wants* us to ask—he earnestly desires us to ask—he requests and commands us to ask. For as we keep on asking, seeking, knocking, we keep our relationship with God alive, vital, and in the present. The daily discipline of directing our specific requests to God allows us to build our relationship with him. As we grow in faith, we will learn other ways to pray to God, such as simply praising him for who he is, adoration and thanksgiving, or confessing where we have failed him and his plan for the Kingdom. In all these ways we will set our minds and hearts in tune with him. But petition, or asking, is one of the closest, simplest, most basic kinds of prayer.

It is God meeting us at the point of our need for him, and this, after all, is what our daily bread represents. That is why God is pleased when we ask for it.

Immediately after teaching the disciples to say, "Give us this day our daily bread," Jesus tells a story of "the importunate friend":

"Then he said to them, 'Suppose one of you has a friend who comes to him in the middle of the night and says, "My friend, lend me three loaves, for a friend of mine on a journey has turned up at my house, and I have nothing to offer him"; and he replies from inside, "Do not bother me. The door is shut for the night; my children and I have gone to bed; and I cannot get up and give you what you want." I tell you that even if he will not provide for him out of friendship, the very shamelessness of the request will make him get up and give him all he needs. And so I say to you, ask, and you will receive; seek, and you will find; knock, and the door will be opened. For everyone who asks receives, he who seeks finds, and to him who knocks, the door will be opened'" (Luke 11:5–10; NEB).

It is important to realize not only that this man was granted his request by his friend because he asked in simple faith, believing in his friend's ability and desire to help him—actually, he embarrassed his friend into helping him!—but also that this man had a good reason for needing the three loaves: another friend was asking him for them!

What resources do you need in order to live *and* to help others? An education, presentable clothing, a place to live, dependable transportation, materials for crafts, money, time, physical energy, a loving and joyful spirit? These are some of the loaves you may receive from your Father—if you ask for them. God not only has the desire to give us our daily bread, he has the ability to give it to us.

When things are going well, we sometimes forget to come to God. We begin to believe we have the world by the tail and our good fortune is all our own doing, thanks to our good breeding, or our associations, or our good looks, or our intelligence. And then something happens—something that irritates us or frightens us or discourages us—and we realize how incredibly helpless we are. We remember who our Father is, and we go running to him for help. There's nothing wrong with that—it's part of being human. But if we never felt helpless or inadequate to meet life's challenges, if we were given everything before we felt the need for it, what kind of relationship would we have with God? We would forget our need —not only for his gifts, but for God himself. Yet he remains the Creator, and we are his children, with a son's or a daughter's right to talk to him about our lives, to depend upon him for all our needs. This relationship is the structure of his creation, and in his love he will never let us forget it.

How easy it is for some of us (me!) to begin to depend on or trust ourselves—our efforts, our experience, our talents— and forget that God is the Giver of all, and the only One worthy of our ultimate trust. Though it often hurts—even humiliates me—I am grateful every time God pulls me up short and reminds me of this basic truth of life in Christ.

John Alexander spoke for me when he wrote: "The heart of the matter is that we are to trust God, not ourselves. Our strength and might are perfectly irrelevant in God's plan. We can do nothing on our own, and God intends for us to learn that."

The children of Israel experienced a day-to-day dependence upon God when Moses led them out of Egypt and slavery. In Exodus 16 we read that about forty-five days after leaving Egypt (the Bible mentions one month and fifteen days), the Israelites came to a wilderness stretching between a delightful oasis with twelve springs and seventy palm trees on one side, and the Sinai Desert on the other side. As the story goes, the Israelites complained to Moses and Aaron: ". . . you have brought us out into this wilderness to let this whole assembly starve to death!" (Exod. 16:3; NEB). Of course, they were wrong. They had been led from the slavery—and security—of

Egyptian society, and now they had to trust God continually for their daily existence. But God did not abandon them. "I will rain down bread from heaven for you," he said to Moses, and he kept his word.

Moses was instructed to tell the people to gather only enough bread, or "manna"—". . . it was white, like coriander seed, and it tasted like a wafer made with honey" (Exod. 16:31; NEB)—for each day, one day at a time, except on the day before the Sabbath when they were to gather enough for two days. The Israelites found that when they gathered the manna as the Lord had instructed, no one had too much to eat and no one had too little. Each "had just as much as he could eat." They also found that if they disobeyed the Lord's instructions and gathered more bread than they needed for the one day, "it became full of maggots and stank" (Exod. 16:20; NEB).

What was true of the Israelites on their way from Egypt to the Promised Land is also true of us in our daily living: we must constantly remember our need for and our dependence upon our heavenly Father as the source of all life, physical and material as well as spiritual.

In John 15 we read: ". . . ask whatever you will, and it shall be done for you. By this my Father is glorified, that you bear much fruit" (vv. 7–8). This tells us another important reason why we must ask God to supply our daily bread. Once we have accepted his Fatherhood, he has fruit for us to bear . . . work for us to do! In Matthew 25 Jesus tells a story about three servants whose master entrusted each of them with different amounts of his gold and told them to invest it while he was away. When the master returned to take an accounting of the investments, he found that the first two servants had doubled his capital and brought him a handsome profit. The master called those two servants "good and trusty," and said to them, "You have proved trustworthy in a small way; I will now put you in charge of something big. Come and share your master's delight!" (NEB). But the third servant, in fear, had simply hidden his master's gold in the ground. The story ends with the master's wrath at that servant, whose fear prevented him even from putting the money in a bank where it could have drawn interest.

By means of this story, Jesus was telling us that God is like that master. He has entrusted us, his servants, with some of his gold—in the form of time, energy, ability, money, experience, and tools—and he wants us to invest it wisely. If we are honestly trying to do the Lord's business, he will also supply whatever else we need to get the job done.

Asking God for what we need, then, is a vital link in the chain of prayer. We ask—and we ask again—and our persistence clarifies our desires. We ask—because in framing our specific daily requests, we are reminded of our dependence on our Creator as we open our hearts to him, allowing him to commune with us. We ask—because the resources we need will enable each of us to do the work God, our Father, has assigned to us. And we ask—because what we need is not only for ourselves, but for the glory of God and his Kingdom . . . for the blessing of his world.

# PART II

## THE CONDITIONS OF ASKING

## Chapter 5

## *But First—Abide*

Anyone who works in a garden knows the sad experience of coming across a shrub or a tree whose branches have been damaged by storms, or someone's careless handling, or any number of accidental bruises. Once the branches are disconnected from the main stem, or vine, they gradually wither, dry up, and die because there is no way they can acquire life-sustaining sap on their own. And we are no different when it comes to our relationship with Jesus Christ. He himself pointed this out when he said: "I am the true vine, . . . you are the branches. He who abides in me, and I in him, he it is that bears much fruit, for apart from me you can do nothing. . . . If you abide in me, and my words abide in you, ask whatever you will, and it shall be done for you. By this my Father is glorified, that you bear much fruit. . . ." (John 15:1–8).

And so, before we can ask for our needs, we must meet certain conditions. There are certain ways in which we must present our petitions if they are to be effective.

*Aha!* you are saying. Then we can't simply ask for something and expect to receive it? Even if we ask in order to serve?

The answer is no because first we must be in a position to serve. We must have the strength and will to serve, and we cannot find these things within ourselves. Only God can supply them to us, and only when—and because—we are abiding in him.

*Abide* is a word we seldom use today, and I think it is because it doesn't fit easily into our busy way of life. We do everything quickly. We move swiftly from one activity to another. Somehow *abide* even sounds as if it requires time.

And so it does. It requires all the time we have in our lives . . . because it means that we *remain, continue, stay, endure, go on being* with our Lord every moment of every hour of every day. In a spiritual sense, *to abide* in Christ is *to be wrapped* in him. We are in him and he is in us, and this is a mystery we must experience to understand.

As Andrew Murray explains it, "Abiding is the acceptance of my position, the consent to be kept there, the surrender of faith to the strong vine still to hold the feeble branch."

If we are not abiding in Christ, then all the tools he could ever supply will not enable us to serve him. For unless we, the branches, are connected to him, our Vine, we will be too weak, too withered and dried up, to be of any ultimate use in this world. "It is the vine that draws the sap from the kindly earth; . . . the vine that enables them even to hold on, in order that they may get more" (The Interpreter's Bible).

Have you ever noticed that when we are trying to do something on our own, we often get in our own way? Our son Dan was talking about this the other day. Dan is a surfer, and has been ever since he was a little guy. In fact, during his high school years he made surfboards and spent part of every day either in or on the sea. But he says that when he was just beginning to surf, occasionally a big wave would knock him off his surfboard and he would be thrown down into the water as if he were in a mixer. In the tumbling and turbulence of a broken wave, a surfer can become disoriented, not knowing which way will lead to the surface. The more he struggles to come up for air, the faster he runs out of breath, and in the confusion may actually be swimming toward the sandy bottom.

As Dan became a more experienced surfer, he learned that the thing to do when he was overpowered by a big wave was to relax—completely. This allowed God's natural forces to work with him, which, in this case, means that the surfer's positive buoyancy will carry him up to the surface of the water.

Dan says that now he often applies this lesson in surfing to his spiritual life. Sometimes, like many of us, he strives too hard to do something he knows is important to Christ—and that is when he trips over his own feet! Then he remembers . . . and relaxes, taking one step at a time, realizing that he can't possibly do everything himself. He will do his part, and others will do theirs, and God will give them all the resources they need to get the job done. The less energy consumed by confused striving, the more easily God can do his work in and through us.

Jesus surely knew what it meant to abide in his Father. Again and again throughout the Gospels we see him withdrawing from people to be with God; and even as he went about his everyday activities he seemed to carry on a running conversation with God in his heart. We can do the same thing —although it will mean arranging our lives in such a way that there is never a moment when we need be out of contact with our Father. Admittedly, that will be difficult, but not impossible, for God does not ask the impossible of us. Here again we come upon the marvelous mystery of his living in us and our living in him: God himself will give us the grace and the power to abide in him. Abiding, in itself, is something we cannot do without him.

We can't help but wonder how we shall manage to do what God asks of us in this sense if abiding means that we must think of God all the time. After all, we have responsibilities: a family to care for, interests to pursue, talents to develop,

ve. If abiding means withdrawing from these con-
uld have to live a cloistered kind of life, and God
ll us away from this world, but, rather, into it. Can
abide in God even in the midst of our everyday
life?

Yes—and there are helps along the way. Brother Lawrence shared his method of abiding in his beautiful book *Practicing the Presence of God*. Even while performing the humblest, most tedious tasks, this committed man was aware of God's nearness. Not that he was *un*aware of the presence and needs of others; he simply kept himself open to God and to the strength that flowed from the Vine into the branch.

We can follow Brother Lawrence's example, no matter where we are or what we are doing. It doesn't mean that we have nothing else on our minds and in our hearts, but that underneath everything else that claims our attention is the steady, constant awareness of God. We keep in spiritual touch with him:

> Speak to Him thou for He hears, and
>    Spirit with Spirit can meet—
> Closer is He than breathing, and nearer
>    than hands and feet.
>                    —Alfred, Lord Tennyson

We do not always think consciously of our hands and feet, or of our breathing, but we know they are there. It is the same with our spiritual knowledge of God.

I am reminded of those times when my husband is away for a few days, and how pleased I am when he calls and says, "Just had a minute between meetings, and wanted to touch base." To me it says that underneath all the busyness of his day, I am on his mind . . . and I feel warm, strengthened, connected.

Abiding is not something that simply happens when we come to Christ. Opening our heart to him is only the beginning of the Christian life. Unless we remain with him, we will miss the joy and blessing that should mark us as his. We will become like those persons who are only Christian enough to be miserable because they have no spiritual sense of the nearness of the Lord. They have come to Christ, but the experience leaves them wanting.

Only through abiding with Christ can we reflect to others the radiance of his love. For even after Christ spoke to the disciples about the need to abide, he said, "These things I have spoken to you, that my joy may be in you, and that your joy may be full" (John 15:11).

If you feel that you are losing the glow you once felt as a Christian—or if you know someone who does—then the reason may be that you are not continuing to be wrapped in Christ as you once were. If you miss the taste of the living water you received through your relationship with him, you can experience it anew each day of your life through abiding.

In our hectic world, it is so easy to become wrapped up in things other than our relationship with God. We may even do ourselves a spiritual disservice through trying to serve him in ways of our own choosing. Frank Laubach dealt with this kind of busyness when he wrote:

"I must pursue this voyage of discovery in quest of God's will. I must because the world needs it. I must plunge into mighty experiments in intercessory prayer, to test my hypothesis that God needs help to do His will for others, and that my prayers release His power. I must be a channel for the world needs me. Clearly, clearly, my job here is not to go down to the town plaza and make proselytes, it is to live, wrapped in God, trembling to this thought, burning with His passion. And, my loved one, that is the best gift you can give to your own town" (*Letters by a Modern Mystic*).

And how many of us will identify with this description of St. Teresa of Ávila struggling with the call of the world:

"One day, trying to become still in the chapel, the saint noticed that the altar hangings were crooked. 'How careless the sacristan is,' she said to herself. 'I must . . . No. I am here to pray, not to tell the sacristan what to do.' With a smile she quieted down, only to hear a sharp noise on the roof where some tiles were being replaced. 'That careless workman!' she thought. 'I had better get out of here. No mere man could do it right. . . . No, not now,' and once more, she returned to rebuild silence" (Morton Kelsey, *The Other Side of Silence*).

Notice that Jesus said we are to abide *in* him. That is very different from abiding *with* someone. We abide with other people and, we hope, have close, nurturing relationships. But even if we do, we cannot abide with others all the time. We come and go, and so do they, and we may experience loneliness when we are apart. Not so when we abide *in* Christ, for there is no way we can then be separated. We become part of him and he becomes part of us.

As Andrew Murray put it: "I am persuaded that neither death with its fears, nor life with its cares, nor things present with their pressing claims, nor things to come with their dark shadows, nor height of joy, nor depth of sorrow, nor any other creature, shall be able, for one single moment, to separate us from the love of God which is in Christ Jesus our Lord, and in which He is teaching me to abide."

We cannot possibly live the way Christ wants us to live unless we learn what it means to abide in him . . . to be the branch to his Vine. Is he saying that we can do nothing on our own? That we are not, and never will be, spiritual do-it-yourselfers? For many of us, that will be hard. For instance, my natural approach to a task is to try doing it on my own, and if I don't succeed, I try harder. But that is not the way to abide in Christ. What, then, is? For the answer, we must ask Christ himself.

Jesus begins this lesson by saying, "I am the true vine," and it seems to me there is a special emphasis on the word *true*. Often, when he was trying to make a point, Jesus spoke in terms of the familiar, of something near at hand with which everyone could identify, and this time was no exception. In Palestine, vines grew everywhere: on terraces, in well-mani-cured gardens, creeping lazily over the ground and framing the doors of humble cottages. Wherever one looked, there was the vine. But it was not only familiar to the eye, it was also part of the religious heritage of Israel, for in the pages of the Old Testament, Israel is often called the vine or the vineyard of the Lord: "Yet I had planted thee a noble vine, wholly a right seed" (Jer. 2:21); "For the vineyard of the Lord of hosts is the house of Israel" (Isa. 5:7); "Thy mother [Israel] is like a vine in thy blood, planted by the waters" (Ezek. 19:10; KJV). Again and again, the nation and the vine are linked, until the vine becomes the symbol of Israel. And it was in this setting that Jesus called attention to the one true Vine—not the nation or anything else, but only God.

Was he telling the Israelites, "Don't make the mistake of thinking that because you belong to Israel and are a member of a chosen people, you are therefore automatically a branch in the vine of God"? And is he saying the same thing to us, today? Is he telling us, "The nation is not the true Vine—I am. . . . Neither your background, your education, your family, your nationality, your wealth, nor any other thing or quality will guarantee you a place in my Kingdom. Only a liv-ing union with me can do that for you . . . for I am the one true Vine, and only when you are joined to me are you joined to God"?

In describing himself as the *true* Vine, Christ intends for us to learn that we are to depend on him—first and most and for everything we need. Anything else upon which we depend for our security, for our strength, even for our lives, is a false vine —and there are many in our world today. We are not a pasto-ral country, like Palestine in the days of Jesus' ministry, and we can't look around and see as many vines as people did then, but they are here, all around us, ever intertwined so subtly in our lives that we often don't recognize them for what they are—the false vines we put before our Lord, the substitutes with which, and with whom, we mistakenly abide and seek to be connected.

We see this in many of our political figures—on both sides and even in the middle—who put their trust in a particular philosophy, believing that it is the only right one by which they, and everybody else, should live. We see it in those who put their trust in social position, or family background, or a superior education, or wealth, or material goods, or achievement. We see it in church members who put their trust in specific dogmas or theological systems rather than in God. We see it in those who find their security in being good church members and carrying out many important projects instead of developing a close, personal relationship with their living Father in heaven.

We even see it in families: in husbands and wives who put each other before God . . . in wives who trust in their husbands to be their vines and unfairly expect them to give them everything they need to live . . . in mothers and fathers who put their children before anything and anyone else, or try to be vines to them and at the same time prevent them from discovering the true Vine. We see it in some women who look for their security in a "me-first" way of life, without regard for others and without seeking God's will for their newly developed abilities. And we have seen it for a long time in men who put their ambitions first.

Yes, there are many false vines, and none of them can nourish us. As long as we keep them in perspective, they have a place in our lives, but when we put them before God, when we try to abide with them rather than in him, he may have to cut them down—not out of anger, but simply to show us that they are not strong enough to support the branch of our lives. Only he can do that. Only he can enable us to live so abundantly, on such a large scale, so joyously and sacrificially that our lives will honor him. It is a matter of trust. We are to trust

God, and God alone, and he means this kind of abiding to come first in our lives.

". . . apart from me you can do nothing" (John 15:5; NEB). This was not meant to humiliate us, but, rather, to turn us toward the magnificent, illimitable source of power Christ offers us. As The Interpreter's Bible says of this verse, ". . . these are surely the most hopeful words in Scripture, for they make so clear the fact that we are not to 'try harder,' but to 'let go, and let God.' Knowing all there is to know, the very worst, he is not daunted in the least, is sure that he can manage for us. Meantime he is not surprised that apart from him, or using him only sporadically, we have not done better. He knew that without him we could do, not something fairly good though insufficient, but just nothing at all. *I am the vine, you are the branches.* And the vine does and must do everything for them. It is the vine that draws the sap from the kindly earth; the vine that passes it to the needy branches; the vine that enables them even to hold on, in order that they may get more. Apart from the vine, the branches are mere withering sticks, soon ready for the burning; and there comes a puff of smoke, a crackle of the fire, and then nothing at all. 'But I,' says Christ, 'can make you green and living things, heavy with fruitfulness, laden with usefulness toward God and man'" (pp. 715–16).

Jesus, our Vine, is our contact, the point at which we interface with God. In him we find our very life, or, as Paul Tillich calls it, "the ground of our being."

As we progress in our life of prayer, there is, says Thomas Merton, an awakening in us of "a consciousness of our union with God, of our complete dependence on Him, for all our vital acts in the spiritual life, and of His constant, loving presence in the depths of our souls." *In the depths of our souls*— yes, here is where we maintain our constant communication with our Creator!

Thomas Merton also reminds us that "contemplation is the

awareness and realization, even in some sense *experience*, of what each Christian obscurely believes: 'It is now no longer I who lives, but Christ who lives within me.' "

When Jesus said, "I am the true vine, . . . you are the branches," he was promising to hold us fast, to feed us, to enable us to grow, and to produce fruit in our lives so that God might be glorified. But what of us? What are we to do? Surely we must give *something* to this relationship?

Indeed we must. Our task is to stay connected, to remain the branches to his Vine.

*That* simple? Yes, but unfortunately we often complicate our task by trying too hard to do it.

Abiding in Christ shouldn't be a strain on our energies. Nor should we have to strive mightily to remain open to Christ so that he can work through us. And yet staying connected isn't something that happens automatically; there *are* steps we must take to achieve it.

*We must make time for God* so that the life of the Vine can flow into the branches and keep the connection strong and vital. How we do that will not be the same for all of us. We can do it through prayer (and we have already discussed the many different ways of praying). We can, in the depths of our soul, maintain a continual awareness of God's presence, as Thomas Merton encouraged us to do. We can play Frank Laubach's game of deliberately spending more minutes of each day in an outward communion with God. We can nourish the habit of practicing the presence of God, as Brother Lawrence did, seeking more and more examples of the ways God reveals himself to us in the world and in the people around us.

*We must be people of the Word.* A branch cannot connect itself—*by* itself—to the Vine, and this is why striving doesn't enable us to abide with God. A branch can only *stay* connected. But as a result of our connectedness with God, we will, simply and naturally, live out the faith that is transmitted to us. We will not merely speak God's Word—we will make it an intrinsic part of our lives. We will, in a sense, become the Word as the Word becomes us . . . and this is what Jesus meant when he said we could ask for anything as long as his words abide in us. People of the Word bear the fruit of the Word.

Living the Christian life, then, is not a means to abiding, but rather a *result* of abiding. This distinction is very important, for God is not telling us to abandon our good works. He is, however, telling us that our good works will grow out of our close relationship with him.

Prayer is both a help in abiding and a result of abiding. As we pray and submit to Christ, our will is lined up with his will, our desires become more nearly his, and this, in turn, is a powerful aid to our continued abiding in him. It is when we abide—and because we abide—that we can ask for anything and have it given to us, because our thoughts and desires are in line with God's. As our will becomes his will, we ask what *we* will.

This is especially true when it comes to God's glory, which is the goal of an abiding life. For, as Andrew Murray says, "Abiding in Christ, the soul learns not only to desire, but spiritually discern what will be for God's glory."

If Christ finds us willing to trust ourselves and our interests to his love, if in that trust we give up all care for our own will and honor, if we make it our glory to exercise and confess absolute dependence on him in all things, if we are content to have no life but our life in him, he will do for us what the Father did for him.

The answers to our prayers will not always come to us immediately: they may be delayed . . . they may come in a form that is different from what we had in mind. God may say no to a particular petition but send us inner peace to deal with our need. Or we may pray for patience and receive tribulation . . . but "tribulation worketh patience" (Rom. 5:3; KJV).

Whatever the need, it will be fulfilled according to God's will and not ours, and if we are truly abiding with him, we will receive our answers with joy.

"If . . . my words abide in you . . ." Perhaps most of us haven't paid much attention to the words that abide in us. Perhaps we don't even consider words as abiding at all, but as little pieces of communication that come and go as quickly as we think of them. But remember: "As he thinketh in his heart, so is he" (Prov. 23:7; KJV). The way we think, the words we use to shape our thoughts—silently or aloud—become part of us. As we invite them into our lives, we must ask ourselves: Are they words of fear, gloom, pessimism? Of gossip and criticism? Are we opening up our hearts and minds to foolish words, negative words, evil words? What words—more important, *whose* words—shape our lives? By whose word concepts do we live?

Jesus said he wants *his* words to abide in us . . . to shape us, to conform us to his image and life-style. And as we read and study his Word we are reminded: "Whatsoever things are true, whatsoever things are honest, whatsoever things are just, whatsoever things are pure, whatsoever things are lovely, whatsoever things are of good report; if there be any virtue, and if there be any praise, think on these things" (Phil. 4:8; KJV). What we think and feel is bound to come out because in a very real sense we are what we think. How important it is, then, for us—in word, thought, and deed—to magnify the Lord, to let our words bless rather than curse.

As people of the word, we are to be "doers of the word, and not hearers only" (James 1:22; KJV). For words are cheap if they are not backed up by deeds. Scripture is one of God's ways of speaking directly to us. It is a channel for the nutrients we receive from the precious Vine, and we must not take our Scripture reading lightly. As we study God's Word, as we memorize portions of it in order to have it with us always, we will begin to change and grow.

I love the story of the missionary who was teaching a group of new converts in India, explaining to them what it meant to live as Christ would. All of this, of course, was very new to the class and they were eager to learn. Then, one day, a young man didn't show up for class. The next day and the next he was absent, and the missionary was concerned. He was afraid the young man had left his newfound faith, or that his family might have put pressure on him to withdraw. But finally the man returned to the class, which greatly relieved the missionary.

"Where have you been all these days?" the missionary asked his student. "I've been worried about you!"

The young man was surprised. "Oh," he said, "I was out applying the things you taught us about the Christian life, I'm back to learn more." Now there was a doer as well as a hearer of the Word!

I have a very strong feeling that the more we pray, the more we will be sent out into life to work out God's will for us. I have seen this happen in many lives, most recently in a wonderful woman named Amy, who became a Christian somewhat late in her life. And as Amy began to abide in her Lord, she found that she was beginning to apply his words to her everyday life. For instance, she found herself having to speak in a different way to friends she had known for years. "I just have to say it like it is," she explained, which was quite a change from the woman she used to be. Amy was known for doing the right thing at all times, for knowing when to speak tactfully and when to keep quiet. Now, to be true to her Lord and herself, there are times she has to put social rules aside. When she is in the presence of gossip or an attitude of exclusivism, she cannot allow it to go unchallenged. If someone asks her opinion, she can no longer say, "Oh, my dear, you're doing the right thing!" if it isn't the right thing. She has to be honest. "The closer I get to the Lord," Amy says, "the more I have to say what I feel is true."

When we ask ourselves, "What would Jesus do?" we are becoming doers of his words, and this is where our study of Scripture should lead us.

*We must praise the Lord.* We are told, "always and for everything" give thanks (Eph. 5:20), and this is not always easy to do. Of course, when things are going well for us, when joy is overflowing, praise comes readily to our lips. But when adversity seems to be the order of the day, when we are depressed and out of fellowship with God, the last thing we want to do is to praise him. But when we do, when we give voice to our gratitude even in the hard times—even as our stubborn wills resist—something amazing happens to us. As we offer God our praise, we find ourselves drawn to him, and in his presence we are changed. Our attitude is transformed, our despondent mood is lifted, and we are open once more to his abiding life within us.

In Isaiah we are told we will be given "the mantle of praise instead of a faint spirit" (61:3). What wonderful medicine!

I remember the early days in the church we served in Bel Air, California. The pace was fast, and sometimes the pressures intense. At those times it was not uncommon for Louie to suffer from painful migraine headaches, and when they came, there didn't seem to be anything he could do except endure them. One evening, just before he was to lead the congregation in worship, he was lying down in a darkened room, his head throbbing, and he felt as if the Lord was saying, "Louie, are you willing to praise me?"

"Praise you?" Louie asked. "Feeling the way I do?"

"Yes."

"All right, Lord," Louie sighed. "I'll do my best." He had to force himself to think about all the blessings in his life, and he mentioned them one by one, praising God for his love and power.

Soon it was time for the Sunday service to begin and Louie left the darkened room and went into the sanctuary, which, in those days, was also our living room. He still had his headache; nevertheless he chose a song of praise to begin the service. As he led the congregation in singing, he began to feel a bit better, and by the time they finished the hymn, his headache was completely gone. Ever since that time, Louie makes a conscious act of the will to praise the Lord "in *all* things"— not only when praise comes easily to his lips.

"The best way to show our gratitude to God and the people is to accept everything with joy," says Mother Teresa of Calcutta. "A joyful heart is the normal result of a heart burning with love. Never let anything so fill you with sorrow as to make you forget the joy of Christ Risen."

*We must labor together.* As we join others who are working with Christ, as we share their burdens and cares, as we contribute our strength and abilities to something important in the building of God's Kingdom, we grow closer to Christ himself. We become part of his body of workers, encouraging one another, witnessing together, "rooted and grounded in love" (Eph. 3:17; KJV).

Some of us are not, by nature, team people. Some of us are more comfortable working alone. There are times when we must and should work alone, but there are also times when only a team can accomplish certain goals for the Lord.

I have known people who shy away from groups and who reluctantly become part of a team. And I have seen the delight in their faces when they experience the thrill of accomplishing something for God—on behalf of the poor and the powerless—along with their brothers and sisters in Christ. I have heard more than one of them say that they came to give and were given unto . . . and through their closer relationship with others, they have been drawn closer to Christ himself.

One of the most beautiful experiences I have known has been participating in the work of an urban ministry called Adopt-a-Block here in Washington, D.C. This is a group of Christians who, under the leadership of John Staggers, are working with residents living in a single block in one of the city's depressed areas. Together we repair and renovate their homes so they can keep them and not lose them to decay and condemnation procedures. Ultimately the urban ministry hopes to buy and renovate old, unused buildings for low-income housing in the area. We are of different races, different churches, and many different cultures, but we are one in Christ, and our fellowship is pure joy.

On a "Work Saturday," a group of us spends all day in our designated block, hammering, painting, cleaning out debris, repairing. . . . The last time we went, I helped paint a bathroom in the home of an eighty-year-old woman, a delightful person who kept our work crew good company as we worked. At the end of the day we meet in the basement of a church on the block and have a wonderful meal together, getting to know our friends in the block much better, singing and laughing and, sometimes, crying—*together*. Let me tell you, *abiding* is something each of us can actually feel in that atmosphere!

*We must be obedient.* John 15:10 sums up this important requisite to abiding in Christ: "If you keep my commandments, you will abide in my love."

And what are Christ's commandments? That we love him with all our heart, soul, strength, and mind . . . and that we love others as we love ourselves.

Obedience was crucial in the relationship Jesus had with his Father, and so it is in our relationship with him. But obedience means more than knowing what the commandments are; it means searching the scriptures for understanding, and then working the commandments out in practical, everyday ways. It is one thing to accept the Gospel intellectually—and quite another to apply it to life. When God's love is working in and through us, it changes the way we think, feel, treat people, and respond to their needs. It changes everything about us— *if* we submit to that love.

And here we come to the matter of "good works." To persons outside of Christ, good works may be a stumbling block that keep them from a life in Christ: they want a relationship based on faith in Christ, not on the things they do for him.

But when we abide in Christ, doing his work becomes an inherent part of the faith relationship we have with him. It is an expression of our love for him and his for us. Good works can never bring us to God, but as we abide in him, we want to serve him and others out of the gratitude of our hearts. We submit to the truth that we are "created in Christ Jesus unto good works" (Eph. 2:10; KJV).

The only way we can really abide in Christ is by faith. "As therefore you received Christ Jesus the Lord, so live in him, rooted and built up in him and established in the faith" (Col. 2:6–7).

*We have the Holy Spirit.* The Holy Spirit is the life sap through which the Vine and branches grow into one. He is the bond of fellowship between Christ and his people and he teaches us to abide. He quickens our faith in the Vine and convinces us we are connected to it. He is, in fact, our *living* connection.

There is no way we can abide with Christ without the help of the Holy Spirit . . . nor are we expected to! For it is the task of the Holy Spirit to make Christ live in us. When Jesus says, "Abide in me," he is offering himself—through the Holy Spirit—in all his power and love.

And so, though we are to respond in obedience and love to his commands, and keep ourselves open to his life in us, the real work of abiding is the Holy Spirit's. When our strength fails us, we have *his* strength to support us. When our faith weakens, we need only open ourselves to the One who is perfectly faithful and trustworthy at all times.

Abiding, then, is not for the "super-religious" who feel no need, who have never stumbled and fallen, whose strength seems to have no end. Abiding is for those of us who are very much in need—and know it!

I love the way Andrew Murray expresses this help we receive from the Holy Spirit: "Abiding in Him is not a work that *we* have to do as the condition for enjoying His salvation, but a consenting to let him do all for us, and in us, and through us."

# Chapter 6

## *In Jesus' Name*

At lunchtime, recently, as a group of us working on an inner-city project relaxed around one member's big oak kitchen table, we began talking about the concerns in our lives. Mostly they involved other members of our families—a husband who lost his job when his company was dissolved, a daughter going through a tough time, elderly relatives struggling to live on a pension that doesn't stretch far enough in today's inflated economy, a friend with a serious illness. It helped each of us to be able to talk freely, knowing we could speak and be heard—in love.

We were all moved by the care and concern we felt for one another, and even though we had prayed at the beginning of our meal, during our conversation we wanted to communicate with God again. So, we joined hands, and each of us brought the needs we had just voiced to God. And as we ended our prayers of petition for one another's needs, each of us said these same words: "In Jesus' name."

Whenever we need anything from the Lord, we use those words. In fact, they have become so much a part of asking prayer that we often say them without realizing what they mean. And that's unfortunate, because although these words come at the end of our petition, they actually represent the very beginning of our asking. By acknowledging God's owner-

ship of our lives, we meet the first condition of our asking—
but unless we can speak "in Jesus' name" honestly, from the
depths of our being, we are not yet ready to do serious business with God.

Most of us probably can't remember how or when we
learned to add "in Jesus' name" to the end of a prayer. Perhaps our parents taught us, or we might have learned it in
church. But that isn't really where these words begin. They
came to us from Jesus himself! "Indeed anything you ask in
my name I will do" (John 14:13; NEB).

Does that mean, then, that a Christian can ask God to
make him rich, healthy, and happy as long as he adds "in
Jesus' name" to the end of his request? Is it a magic phrase
entitling us to lavish rewards? Can we use it to avoid the trou-
bles of life? Some people seem to think so, only to be disappointed when such rewards are not given. To paraphrase
James, they ask amiss (4:3)—and when we ask amiss, it is a
bit like talking to the wall, or mouthing words without making a sound.

"In Jesus' name" is not a key to a treasure chest; it is an expression of a spiritual responsibility that accompanies us
whenever we come to God in our need. It means first that we
are his, and then that we are asking him for the kind of things
Christ would want if he were in our situation. It says, "Lord,
we are asking as your Son would ask. We are yours, and want
to serve you as he served. We want to know your mind, and
do your will."

But how can we know God's mind? Can we ordinary
human beings project ourselves into the mind of God? If we
believe we can, we are making the same mistake Adam and
Eve made when they believed the serpent's seductive promise,
". . . you shall be as gods, and know . . ." (Gen. 3:5).

The gap between our mind and God's mind is far too vast
for us to bridge. We tried to reach God with our own intelligence, and we failed. That is one of the reasons Christ came

to us: to be the liaison, the living connection between God and his people.

Only Jesus understands the mind of God. Only he can tell us what we are to do in the Kingdom, or for what special purpose God created us. Any other source of information can only become a guessing game. But in order to learn these terribly important secrets, we must live close to Jesus, so close that even our own will cannot get between him and us.

So we have to make a choice, because two wills cannot rule equally in the same being. We cannot serve God *and* our own purposes—we must put either his purposes or ours aside. And only if we choose to accept God's ownership of our lives, believing that he does not rent us, he owns us, can we speak the words "in Jesus' name" truly and sincerely. Only then can we safely ask for "anything," because when we allow Christ to direct our lives, when we begin to live and think as he would, we can grow in the trust that we will not petition God selfishly. For example, we will not ask to be rich and comfortable at the expense of others. We will ask only to receive what we need to live—to serve—and to share—to the praise of *his* glory.

What we are describing is a relationship, which carries with it both rights and responsibilities. But without these elements there cannot be a relationship at all.

Sometimes, however, we may think we are earnestly asking for the things God wants, and *still* run into competition from our own misguided desires. We may come to God as St. Augustine's mother, Monica, did when her son was about to leave home. Monica was a dedicated servant of the Lord, and for years her constant petition was that her son would become a Christian so that he, too, could serve him. For years, Monica's son resisted her urging and the power of her prayers, and finally, at age twenty-nine, said he was going to Rome, where, in his mother's mind, there were such evil and corruption to tempt a young man. Surely, Monica thought, he would be lost—to her and to God—so she asked God to keep her son at home where she could watch (and pray) over him. But God didn't comply, and even as Monica prayed, Augustine sailed for Rome, and later to Milan, where, much to his mother's astonishment, he met St. Ambrose, the bishop "known to the whole world as among the best of men," who was God's instrument in bringing Augustine to Christ (*Confessions,* Book V).

Do you see what Monica was doing? As honestly as she had served God all her life, she couldn't help injecting her own will into her prayers when she was faced with her son's departure. She couldn't quite trust God to bring about his will in his own way and in his own time—she wanted to help him out. Can't you just hear God saying, "It's all right, Monica, thanks for your offer of help, but I'll manage?" Perhaps mothers in particular are vulnerable to this temptation. In his *Confessions,* St. Augustine suggests that God took into account Monica's basic desire—to see her son know God—and so answered the intent and desire of her heart rather than the words that had gone amiss.

Sometimes learning the mind of Christ can be quite a surprise, especially when it turns out to be so different from our own. But this is the way we can gain insight into a person or a situation that otherwise confuses us.

Very often God's way is so different from our own—which is why it is so important for us to pray for an insight into his mind before we ask him for the resources to do his work. Imagine how frustrated and disappointed the disciples must have been when Jesus, under interrogation by Pilate, said, "My kingdom is not of this world; if my kingship were of this world, my servants would fight, that I might not be handed over . . ." (John 18:36). The disciples wanted a military king who would lead them in battle against the oppressive Romans, and it was very hard for them to put that idea aside. In Gethsemane, when Jesus was arrested, Peter had drawn his sword and cut off a soldier's ear—he was more than willing to give up his life fighting for his Master and for his nation's freedom. But Jesus stopped him, saying, "No more of this!" (Luke 22:51), and healed the soldier's wound with a touch of his hand. Many times during his ministry, Jesus had tried to prepare his disciples for this hour of darkness, but they had resisted learning what was in his mind because it was so different from their own desires. Only after the Crucifixion and the Resurrection did they begin to understand, and that was when they were able to ask God for the resources they needed to "make disciples of all nations" (Matt. 28:19).

I have a friend who recently lost her job for reasons that seemed to her very unfair. And in her anguish she began asking God to punish her persecutors. In her mind she thought it would be fitting if her superiors somehow were to lose *their* jobs—but she was astonished when, during a moment of deep prayer, God revealed that he had other thoughts in his mind. He would administer justice—not punishment—in his own way and in his own time, but it was more important then for my friend to learn forgiveness. "You know, that never occurred to me," she told me, "but it was clearly God's way. Because now I have a sense of peace inside me, and I can go on to a more constructive way of living."

God always answers in the way that is best, even when we can't understand his reasons at the time. He can see much farther down the road than we can. After all, if he owns us, he is certainly very much concerned about the development and protection of his property! Our very character and the spirit part of us that will live forever are being shaped by our responses to the circumstances he ordains and allows. We learn to say along with King David, "The Lord will perfect that which concerneth me" (Ps. 138:8; KJV).

A young man I know was humbled by this discovery after he tried to impose his own will upon God because he thought he knew better. Ken never got along well with his father, and saw very little of him. He had bitter memories of his father as an irresponsible, flighty, immature man whose extravagant tastes made life very hard for Ken's mother and his two sisters. One day Ken learned that his father had been in a serious automobile accident and was in the hospital, asking for him. When Ken went to him, his father's doctors said they would have to operate the next morning in an attempt to save the man's life. But even if they were successful, Ken's father would lose a leg.

"My father was such a dependent person, such a child, really," Ken said. "I couldn't imagine him facing life with only one leg—he didn't have that kind of strength. So I asked God to please take him and not let him live. I begged God to spare him any pain. Maybe that was a terrible thing to do, but I knew my father."

But God knew Ken's father better. The man lived. And he surprised everyone with the courage he found to cope with life as a handicapped person. Gone were the childishness, the irresponsibility, the dependence; instead, he insisted on learning to walk with the aid of a prosthesis and a cane, and somehow, through his struggle, he gained the sensitivity and understanding he had lacked all his life. Ken learned to admire him for his determination, and a relationship finally began to form between a father and son. "I guess my father had hidden strengths only God could see," Ken said later. "And maybe that's true of us all."

Sometimes it is tempting to try to replace God's will with our own, and when that happens we can be sure we are not living in that close, connected, branch-in-the-vine relationship with God. This is more likely to occur when we aren't exactly happy to do God's will because it may inconvenience us. Perhaps we are in a destructive relationship with another person, yet we go on allowing it to develop because it's easier than breaking it off or working out the problems—and we resist hearing God telling us to hand over the relationship to him. Or perhaps we realize that God wants us to stop our careless consumption of the earth's resources, yet we are reluctant to give up our affluent way of life—so we give lip service to conservation policies without putting them into practice. We may pray for the hungry without making any attempt to share our food with them. We may withhold comfort from friends who are distressed or confused over a tragedy, because it is inconvenient to give them the time and attention they need. We may refuse to give to a charity at our front door because "we already gave at the office." Perhaps none of these examples fit your situation at the moment, but isn't there something God is telling you to do?—and aren't you hoping he can't possibly mean *that?*

"In Jesus' name" means that we are asking not only for our own nourishment, but for others as well. And what we give out of what we receive says a great deal—not only about who we are, but *whose* we are.

The choice between serving God's will and our own has to be made many times in our lives, and never more often than now, when it is becoming increasingly clear that God wants us to keep less of our daily bread for ourselves. Yes, we can ask for anything if we can ask "in Jesus' name." We can say these words if the ownership of our lives has been settled. If by conscious choice our will has become one with Christ's will, we will grow to want the same things he wants, and we will surely receive it all in his name. "And it is in God's power to provide you richly with every good gift; thus you will have ample means in yourselves to meet each and every situation, with enough and to spare for every good cause" (2 Cor. 9:8; NEB).

## Chapter 7

## The "Nevertheless" Prayer

There are times when God's will is clear and unmistakable and we have no need to ask what it is he wants us to do. We know, for instance, that he wants us always to love our neighbor as ourself, to tell the truth to one another, and to be faithful to him, whatever the cost. So when these particular situations arise, there is no need to wonder "if it be thy will, Lord."

But there are other times when we are not sure what God wants us to do. Often we get into situations where what is right is not so clear, or where what we want finds no outlet. Then we must gather our courage about us and pray the "nevertheless" prayer. This is a basic part of asking prayer and is one of our responsibilities in our relationship with our heavenly Father. It expresses our attitude of submission to his larger power and our trust in his goodness.

Even Jesus came to a point in his earthly life when he was not certain he understood what God wanted for him. Could his good and loving Father *really* want him to experience the agony of the cross? Although he was convinced of his mission "to seek and save the lost," yet Jesus must have shuddered at the thought of a Roman crucifixion, which looked inevitable as he faced those last hours before the Jewish Passover feast. And so he prayed, "O my Father, if it be possible, let this cup pass from me: nevertheless not as I will, but as thou wilt"

(Matt. 26:39; KJV). So great were his anguish and dismay in the struggle to submit himself to God's will that drops of blood appeared on his face. Yet he submitted and endured the cross.

In all our asking prayers, we ask "in Jesus' name." Then we ask for help in discovering the mind of Christ, because we realize that we may only *think* it is the same as ours—and we want to be certain we are in agreement with his desires. But each of us, in our own way and at certain crucial times in our lives, must also be willing to say the "nevertheless" prayer, the prayer that tells our Father we are willing to carry out his desires even if we find that very difficult to do, even if we don't understand why he may want such a course of action from us. And we must be willing to mean every word of that prayer, no matter how bitter they may taste. The experience of submission that follows the "nevertheless" prayer may be hard, but we will have the wonderful satisfaction of knowing that we are obeying the will of God. And by that obedience we show him that we are his children.

How do we know that we are obeying God's will? Before God can give us what we ask of him, he must know that we are his. The "nevertheless" prayer is our way of telling him that no matter what he wants of us, we will obey. It tells him —and reminds us—that we are not dictating to him, that despite our own desires, his desire for us is most important to us. Sometimes it is very hard for us to reach this attitude. Or so it has been for me.

Early in our marriage, Louie and I were absolutely certain for several years that God wanted us to serve in the mission field, and we even knew *which* field. If anyone asked us about our future plans we never prefaced our response with "we think" or "we hope." It was always, positively, "We're going to Africa!" During our seminary years we learned everything we possibly could about Africa and its various cultures. We made many African student friends who shared with us their perceptions of the needs and life-styles of their people. We spent two additional years in preparation by studying in Scotland, and all the while our dream grew in our minds and hearts.

Finally, our student days over, we returned from Scotland and went straight to our Mission Board in New York. Eager and expectant, we offered ourselves in the attitude of "Here we are! Where would you like us to begin?"

The answer, given with gentleness and understanding, was that there wasn't going to *be* any beginning, at least not in Africa. The Mission Board, short on funds, was filling positions only on the basis of absolute need, and that year the need in Africa was for a doctor and a nurse. We didn't qualify.

Stunned, Louie and I went back to our hotel. We were confused. We couldn't understand how such a thing could happen. Had God forgotten about us? Didn't he remember his plans for our lives? We were almost sick with disappointment.

Then, slowly, as the days passed and our disappointment gave way to some insight, it occurred to us that perhaps our will and God's were not, after all, the same. Could it be that there had been some confusion in our communication with him? Had our love for Africa and its people, and our enthusiasm to serve and contribute there, influenced our awareness of God's direction for our lives?

As we prayed in the days that followed, we had the sense of beginning all over again. We knew the important thing was to serve God, and we simply had to find out how he wanted us to do it. "All right, Lord, you must have something else in mind," we prayed. "Could it possibly be something here in the United States? Perhaps something in the inner city?"

Louie and I had always felt drawn to the city and its special needs. Was this natural empathy the Lord's way of leading us? The more we prayed about it, the more we felt that this time we were right.

Our spirits were high all the way back home, where we went straight to our church leaders in Los Angeles. Once again, confident, we offered ourselves, ready to get to work immediately. And once again there was that moment of strained silence, that unmistakable reluctance to speak the words everyone knew we did not want to hear.

"That's very interesting," one of the board members said when we told them what we wanted to do. "But would you consider something *we* want you to do?" Puzzled, Louie and I looked at each other and nodded. The board member continued, "Would you be willing to start a new church?"

Not wanting to close his mind, Louie said he would at least be willing to *talk* about it.

So, while I kept our two small sons in tow, the Presbytery staff member whose responsibility it was to oversee the founding of new churches presented a challenge to Louie and drove him to the neighborhood where a new church was needed— not to the strife-torn inner city of Los Angeles, but high up in the surrounding suburbs, to the beautiful hills of Bel Air, one of the nation's most affluent communities!

When Louie returned from the interview, his expression was a mixture of bewilderment and, in spite of himself, excitement. "Honey, you'll never believe what happened!" he said.

"Don't tell me," I answered, "you feel called to start the new church in Bel Air! Isn't that just like the Lord!" I didn't know whether to laugh or to cry—so I did both. All our earthly belongings were packed neatly in barrels, prepared for a call to Africa that was not offered to us. We had been so absolutely human in our desire to serve in a specific way and place that we never gave God a chance to spell out the details of what *he* had in mind for us. He had to keep closing doors on the opportunities we sought until finally we were almost forced to see—and receive—the opportunity he had specifically designed for us all along.

Africa wasn't easy to give up; nor was the inner city. They had been dreams for too long. And Bel Air, overlooking as it did the city where both of us had grown up, didn't seem like much of a mission field to Louie and me. Why, when we were willing to dare so much, and go so far for God, did he ask us to "restrict" our vision?

God was revealing his will, but we were not eager to bend to it. We couldn't pretend otherwise, so when we came to the Lord in prayer, we told him how disappointed we were. And as we prayed, we began to understand that when we say we will give ourselves to the Lord, he takes us at our word. Our very lives are his to engineer and direct. And so the afternoon came when Louie and I were able, finally, to pray our first real "nevertheless" prayer: "All right, Lord, not our will, but yours, be done."

And then God began to surprise us. In a sense we did become missionaries in Bel Air, helping to give birth to a new church with some of God's salt-of-the-earth people. It was one of the richest experiences of our lives. We learned, too, that there is no place in the world where God is not needed, and no place where the riches of his grace are already spread *too* lavishly.

And Africa? We still dream of going there—but, for now, we love the city of Washington, where God has put us for *this* season of our lives. Perhaps Africa will have to wait until we retire—unless the Lord has other things in mind for us then. He may have—and we may pray the "nevertheless" prayer again, as we have done many times. The prayer is easier for us now, because we have experienced the joy of allowing the great Architect to draw and perfect the plans he desires for each stage of our lives.

Still, there may seem to be a conflict here for you. What of Christ's promises: "Indeed anything you ask in my name I will do, so that the Father may be glorified in the Son. If you ask anything in my name I will do it" (John 14:13–14; NEB), and "If you dwell in me, and my words dwell in you, ask what you will, and you shall have it. This is my Father's glory, that you may bear fruit in plenty and so be my disciples" (John 15:7–8; NEB)?

Why, in the light of these promises, you might be tempted

to wonder, is your specific prayer unanswered, as was our specific prayer to serve in Africa? We did ask in Christ's name, and, as far as we knew, we were abiding in him and he in us.

George Buttrick, in his powerful little book *Prayer,* can help us with what appears to be a confusing relationship. He says that although Christ's promises and assurances concerning petitionary prayer are great and powerful—"wide as time and eternity"—they *always* carry a condition. We can ask anything—*if* we ask in his name, and *if* we abide in him and he in us. But there is even a further condition in Christ's reasons for doing whatever we ask: we must be willing to bear fruit and to glorify God, and we (being created and limited) are not the best judges of how we shall do these things, or where and in what situations we will bear the best fruit for him. That is why some of our petitions go unanswered—and why we have to come to the "nevertheless" prayer.

Our asking prayers have opened us up to ourselves and to God, and in the openness and trust of that relationship we will eventually find the answers we seek. Because of our limited knowledge, we have to keep learning *how* to pray.

God often seems elusive and mysterious, not because he means to confuse us, but because he is so powerful and so all-knowing that we cannot possibly comprehend all of him. But we have not been asked to master him, or to know him completely, or to demand proofs of his strength. We are merely asked to align our will to his will, so that some of his immense power and love can flow through us and his knowledge can direct our lives. Often it will take great courage to do this because God's will may be far more demanding of us than we are of ourselves.

It always comes back to the question: Do we trust God enough to obey him? We may, like Christ, have to take up a cross we truly do not wish to bear. If our intention is to serve the Lord, and if our desire is to enjoy a relationship with him,

we cannot honestly ask for "anything" unless w
pray, ". . . nevertheless not my will, but thine

The hidden blessings to be found in the
prayer are nowhere more eloquently writte
prayer, attributed to a Confederate soldier:

I asked God for strength, that I might achieve.
  I was made weak, that I might learn humbly to obey.
I asked for health, that I might do greater things.
  I was given infirmity, that I might do better things.
I asked for riches, that I might be happy.
  I was given poverty, that I might be wise.
I asked for power, that I might have the praise of men.
  I was given weakness, that I might feel the need of God.
I asked for all things, that I might enjoy life.
  I was given life, that I might enjoy all things.
I got nothing that I asked for—but everything that I had hoped for.
  Almost despite myself, my unspoken prayers were answered.
I am among all men most richly blessed.

## Chapter 8

## *The Prayer of Faith*

A minister I know was once introduced to a woman at a dinner party. "Oh, I'm so happy to meet you," the woman exclaimed. "I'm an admirer of your work!"

When the minister looked a bit puzzled, the woman went on, "Well—you're a man of faith, aren't you? I think faith is the most important thing in the world today—when there's such terrible doubt and uncertainty. You see, I'm a woman of *great* faith!"

The minister nodded, responding, "What is your faith *in?*"

She hesitated. "Why—in faith, I suppose. Yes! I have faith in faith!"

Perhaps what she really meant was that she believed in optimism, or a pleasant feeling that tells us everything is going to work out just fine, although it never tells us why. And then, when something perversely goes wrong, the optimism vanishes because it has no foundation in reality. It has only the strength of a sentiment rather than a way of life.

Faith—the kind Jesus was talking about when he said, "believe in God"—is not an otherworldly, ethereal blissfulness or a cheery hope for the best. Faith looks squarely at life, is able to accept all parts of it, good and bad, and is neither intoxicated by the good times nor frightened into despair by the bad. This kind of faith can accept and manage both the good and the bad because it has an unending source of truth, and love, and power to make good its hope: its object is God. Faith is an attitude of attention and trust based on the character of God.

By itself, faith can do nothing—one may as well grunt as pray. But through its object, God, it can do everything. Without faith, without this attitude of believing attention, it is impossible to know God or what he wants, or to please him.

Faith has always been difficult for us to understand because of its seemingly mysterious power. All of the many miracles Jesus did while he lived on earth—done out of compassion and to convince his disciples, both then and now, of his relationship with God the Father—were done by faith. The very spirit of Jesus, which comes to dwell in us when we invite him, enables us to perform the miracle of the prayer of faith. When Jesus raised a man who had been dead for four days . . . when he made a man see who had been blind from his birth . . . when he provided lunch for over five thousand people out of five small loaves and two small fishes . . . when he turned huge stone jars of foot-washing water into the choicest of wines . . . he wasn't using magic. He was using his power, which was faith.

There is a story in the Gospel of Mark that has always intrigued me. Jesus comes upon a fig tree one day. He is tired from his journey, and hungry. Even though it is not the fig-bearing season, Jesus appears to be angry that the tree has no fruit for him, and he says to the tree, "May no one ever again eat fruit from you!" (Mark 11:12–14; NEB). The next day, Peter and the other disciples see the tree that Jesus cursed, and it is withered from the roots up. Hearing them comment on this event, Jesus says, "Have faith in God. I tell you this: if anyone says to this mountain, 'Be lifted from your place and hurled into the sea,' and has no inward doubts, but believes that what he says is happening, it will be done for him. I tell you, then, whatever you ask for in prayer, believe that you have received it and it will be yours" (Mark 11:20–24; NEB).

I believe that Jesus used dramatically vivid language to tell us that our faith should not be based only on the status quo, or on what we can see with our eyes and touch with our hands. The prayer of faith activates unheard-of and unseen things. In his own life, Jesus never prayed or used the power of God to his advantage, but was completely obedient to the will of his Father. He was trying to tell his disciples, through his response to the fig tree, that their faith in God was sadly too small, and that they had not even begun to realize the resources at their disposal through the prayer of faith. Jesus' own confidence was in a loving heavenly Father who ruled over the physical world, and who waits for his people to work with him, through prayer, to bring his Kingdom to earth. The basis for Jesus' faith, and ours, is trust in our heavenly Father. The believing prayer cannot take place outside of that relationship.

Being naturally curious, we always want to know *how* the miracles happened—and still happen. But there is no *how* in faith: it simply is. But that word *simply* is very important—in order to experience genuine mountain-moving faith, we have to approach God simply, in an attitude of childlike trust.

While reading the life of George Muller recently, I came across a beautiful example of simple faith in God that encouraged me very much. The story comes from the captain of a ship on which George Muller was a passenger. The ship, on its way across the Atlantic to Canada, was slowed down by a thick fog, and the captain had been on the bridge for twenty-two hours.

"I was startled by someone tapping me on the shoulder," the captain wrote. "It was George Muller.

" 'Captain,' said he, 'I have come to tell you that I must be in Quebec on Saturday afternoon.' This was Wednesday.

" 'It is impossible,' I said.

" 'Very well, if your ship can't take me, God will find some other means of locomotion to take me. I have never broken an engagement in fifty-seven years.'

" 'I would willingly help you, but how can I? I am helpless.'

" 'Let us go down to the chart room and pray,' he said.

"I looked at this man and I thought to myself, 'What lunatic asylum could the man have come from? I never heard of such a thing.'

" 'Mr. Muller,' I said, 'do you know how dense this fog is?'

" 'No,' he replied, 'my eye is not on the density of the fog, but on the living God, who controls every circumstance of my life.'

"He went down on his knees, and he prayed one of the most simple prayers. I thought to myself, 'That would suit a children's class where the children were not more than eight or nine years of age.' The burden of his prayer was something like this: 'O Lord, if it is consistent with Thy will, please remove this fog in five minutes. You know the engagement You made for me in Quebec for Saturday. I believe it is Your will.'

"When he had finished, I was going to pray, but he put his hand on my shoulder, and told me not to pray.

" 'First,' he said, 'you do not believe God will do it: and second, I believe He has done it. And there is no need whatever for you to pray about it. . . . Get up, Captain, and open the door, and you will find the fog is gone.'

"I got up, and the fog *was* gone. On Saturday afternoon, George Muller was in Quebec" (from *George Mueller, Man of Faith*).

Simple, childlike faith is one of the conditions of asking prayer. Is our attitude one of defiance, or of challenging God to "prove it"? Or do we come to him like a well-loved son or daughter, asking simply for something that is needed?

Jesus said, ". . . whatever you ask for in prayer, believe that you have received it and it will be yours" (Mark 11:24; NEB). When we allow our attitude to be ruled by doubt—

disbelieving either God's ability or his willingness to help us
—our faith loses touch with its object. Then we miss God's
power and love and knowledge flowing through us. But simple, childlike faith carries with it the reminder that what we
think might be a negative answer from God—a no—is only
one fragment of a heavenly Father's large answer of "Yes!" to
our best well-being.

One of the examples of faith that I love best is found in the
book of Dr. Luke. Jesus met some Jewish elders one day on
his way to the town of Capernaum. They carried a message
from a high-ranking Roman soldier, one who was known to
love Israel, and who had even built the townspeople a meeting
place at his own expense. This centurion had a servant whom
he valued very highly. There must have been a strong relationship between the soldier and his servant, because the servant was a bondservant, meaning one who had of his own free
will consented to remain a servant after having been granted
his freedom. But this servant was very sick now, and even at
the point of death. The message which the Jewish elders
carried from the Roman centurion was that Jesus should
hurry and come to make his servant well. On the way to the
centurion's home, Jesus met up with yet more of the Roman
soldier's friends, who carried a most remarkable message from
him: "Do not trouble further, sir; it is not for me to have you
under my roof, and that is why I did not presume to approach
you in person. *But say the word and my servant will be cured.*
I know, for in my position I am myself under orders, with sol-
diers under me. I say to one, "Go," and he goes; to another,
"Come here," and he comes; and to my servant, "Do this,"
and he does it."

Jesus, amazed at this man's faith, said, "Nowhere, even in
Israel, have I found faith like this"—and the soldier's servant
was totally healed (Luke 7:1–10; NEB). The centurion was
not at all interested in testing Jesus' faith. He realized, from
his own experience of legitimate authority, that Jesus' power
to heal was real, and he trusted in it. He knew Jesus was able

to make the sick healthy once again—not by magic, but simply as a response from one who could help to one who needed it and asked for it. No longer should we wonder, "Can God do it?" but rather, "Can we believe he can?"

As our faith is tested and rewarded, our expectations will grow. For faith needs exercise, or it will become weak, like a muscle that isn't used regularly. God cannot give us our daily bread unless our hands of faith are reaching out to him for it.

The hard thing to understand, however, is that faith is the one area in our lives where growing up means we must grow to be more like a child, trusting simply in the goodness and complete knowledge of a Father who has our best interests at heart. Without this childlike heart of trust in asking prayer—without faith—it is impossible to please God.

# PART III

# WHAT WE CAN ASK FOR

## Chapter 9

## *This Inner Hunger*

There was a time in my late teens when I thought I had everything I needed. I felt very blessed. I had good people in my life—a wonderful mother and close friends. I was healthy, and I had just embarked on a stimulating career in films.

And yet, with all these blessings, I sensed the absence of something. I couldn't define it, but something important was missing on the inside of my life. It wasn't visible to anyone else, but I knew it wasn't there. I had so much to be grateful for that I felt a little guilty for expecting more out of life. Nevertheless, that inner lack made me feel restless, uncertain, and lonely, even among my friends. I told myself I had no right to feel that way—but I was wrong. The emptiness was there—designed by God—and made only to be filled with his presence. Wonderfully, a short time later, that emptiness *did* become filled when I yielded my life to Jesus Christ.

The loneliness, this inner aching, this indefinable sense that something vital to life is missing, is the greatest need a person can have, and only one kind of heavenly provision can fill it. This spiritual hunger can be fed only by Jesus Christ, the Son of God, who called himself the Bread of Heaven.

As he explained to his first disciples, Jesus tells us: "I tell you this: the truth is, not that Moses gave you the bread from heaven, but that my Father gives you the real bread from heaven. The bread that God gives comes down from heaven and brings life to the world" (John 6:32–33; NEB). Later he told them: "I am the bread of life. Your forefathers ate the manna in the desert and they are dead. I am speaking of the bread that comes down from heaven, which a man may eat, and never die. I am that living bread which has come down from heaven; if anyone eats this bread he shall live for ever. Moreover, the bread which I will give is my own flesh; I give it for the life of the world" (John 6:48–51; NEB).

This bread is God's greatest gift to all of us, and we have only to accept it. By receiving and eating the bread from heaven, we become recipients of all the spiritual resources we need. The bread of heaven is the most important spiritual resource we can ask for, and the source of all the others, for by eating it we receive Christ's very life, the new life, the everlasting life that Jesus came to earth to make possible for us to share. He offers himself—his life—as a spiritual loaf for the whole world.

In an eleventh-century Irish illuminated manuscript we find the prayer "Give us today for bread the Word of God from heaven." As we grow into adulthood and old age, our physical life resources will gradually lose their potency and usefulness, and our physical life will eventually cease. But not so with the resources of the spiritual life: faith, hope, and love are gifts that will outlast time itself! And God's word will last forever (1 Cor. 13:13, 1 Pet. 1:22–25).

"If you, then, bad as you are, know how to give your children what is good for them, how much more will your heavenly Father give good things to those who ask him!" (Matt. 7:11; NEB). These "good things" which our heavenly Father gives include love, peace, goodness, meekness, self-control, and patience. We receive them from God through his Holy Spirit, who lives in us as daily we draw nourishment from his word of life. And these good things in turn nourish others—in their spirit (Gal. 5:22–25).

There is only one potential problem. The spiritual bread from heaven—like the manna given to the children of Israel —does not keep overnight and therefore cannot be stored. We must receive it day by day. We cannot wrap it in our parents' spiritual enthusiasm, or even in ours of yesterday. Each day we must have a new willingness to ask for the spiritual resources we need in order to serve our Lord. Opening our hearts up daily, we will gain a new and more acute sensitivity to the hunger in other lives for the bread from heaven. Each day we must decide again to share what we have been given, so that our daily bread may be passed to other hungry hearts.

When Jesus filled that emptiness in my life, I knew how King David must have felt when he sang, "Create a pure heart in me, O God, and give me a new and steadfast spirit" (Ps. 51:10; NEB). I was aware then of an enormous well of love that seemed to spring up out of me and flow toward everyone I knew. That was, and is, the most joyous, energizing emotion I have ever known. All of us who know Christ must have experienced that sensation. It comes from being close to our first and greatest love. We know the joy of asking for—and receiving—the life of Christ himself.

But sometimes, without our being aware of it, we allow our hearts to wander from our first love, and we lose that sense of fulfillment and our first enthusiasm to do God's will on earth. We may even take the love of Christ for granted. That is when the bread of heaven can go stale. We may say the "right" religious words, but our hearts are not right because we are not feeding on the fresh daily bread. All the "right" words turn around and accuse us, because we have become "professional Christians." Our lives are stale, undernourished, and unnourishing.

I like to be around new Christians because they help my heart stay fresh and tender. Bill was that way—he was a man in his early fifties when Louie and I met him and his wife, and he had only recently encountered Christ. But his relationship with his Lord was like the grapes that linger long on the vines —they are the sweetest ones.

All of his life Bill had worked hard and successfully, and he was very wealthy. He had also been an alcoholic for many of those years, and all his money couldn't help him gain control of that inner demon. When Bill became a Christian, he stopped drinking, although he never forgot the pain of the past. "Now I'm a dry alcoholic," he used to say, reminding himself that the temptation and the weakness were still there, kept at a distance only by the strength of God's love.

We knew Bill for years, and in all that time it seemed to us that his love of Christ remained as fresh and new as the moment it began. Surely God created in him a new heart every day. He took nothing for granted: he believed everything God promised, and it seemed to us he served with 100 percent of himself.

One day Bill told us that he wasn't comfortable with all the money he had because he knew so many other people didn't have enough to eat, or decent homes in which to live. Bill didn't decide to give everything away and become a poor man himself. He had a wife and children who depended upon him, and he provided well for them. He also provided a comfortable future for his family. "Now, that comes to about 10 percent of what I have," he said. "We can live on that and give the other 90 percent away."

We have never known anyone who gave away so much in proportion to what he had received. Nor have we ever known anyone who had such a good time doing it! Bill didn't take a lump sum and give it to a person or an organization. He was his own administrator, and giving became his spiritual mission in life. When he saw that someone had a need, he gave. He responded to human needs in all parts of the world, and always anonymously—"In Jesus' name." He gave to enable evangelistic and prayer crusades. He gave to causes dedicated to helping the poor and powerless. He gave to groups working for equal justice for all people. He was a true disciple in that life meant the living out of his faith.

Even Bill's private life was changed by his enthusiastic sharing. The big house where he and his wife lived with their children became filled again with the added voices of adopted children, and from a different racial background. Every time we saw Bill and his wife, we came away feeling blessed and helped by the "first love" so evident in their home and hearts.

Bill had a short discipleship. He died about ten years after he became a Christian, but in those years—like the late grapes—he made up for the "lost time" of his earlier life. And we still feel the inspiration of Bill's stewardship in our lives.

The newness of our first knowledge of Christ is heady wine as we are caught up in our love for him. As we receive the bread of life he gives to us through the Holy Spirit, we are eager to pass it on to others. No need is too great! But, sadly, I suppose it's part of being human to begin taking that marvelous receiving and giving for granted after a while. We're in such a hurry to do our earthly tasks that we gradually fail to seek the daily nourishment we need. We forget where the source of our spiritual life is, and little by little we lose that first sense of joy—until we meet someone like Bill. And then we remember that God has promised to bless us with "all spiritual blessings . . . in Christ"—and that he means to do it *daily* (Eph. 1:3, KJV).

Can you believe it? There is *no* spiritual blessing that may not be ours in Christ. Whatever we need is there for us, and all we have to do is reach out and claim it through prayer. The price has already been paid—by Christ.

A heart genuinely in touch with its first love meets each day as if Jesus had just come into it. It reaches out to those who hunger, thirst, and are lonely. It is sensitive to their pain and gives to their need with whatever it has, confident that its own supply will be replenished. Each day we can receive our living bread from heaven and then offer the overflow to other human beings. And as our hands reach out to meet their waiting hands, we are giving of our love along with the bread.

O Lord, create in me—each day of my life—a new heart, fresh with that first new love of Jesus. *Amen.*

## Chapter 10

## *Lord, Is It Okay to Pray for Money?*

"I'm uncomfortable asking God for money," a friend of mine said. She didn't want it for herself; she wanted to buy and renovate an old house into apartments she could rent out to low-income families who are suffering displacement from what is called by some the regentrification of our city. Mortgage money was tight, and my friend needed a down payment that was bigger than her savings account. Still, she didn't feel right telling God about it.

A young man I know wants to become a medical missionary, which requires years of training in both medicine and theology. That's an expensive proposition, and the young man simply doesn't have the money to accomplish it. "Maybe there's a way to do it," he says, "but I can't bring myself to ask God for the funds I need. It seems selfish of me when you consider all the other needs in this world."

An elderly couple, living on a small, fixed income, just had their rent raised. As carefully as they shop, their food costs keep going up. "We don't know what's going to happen to us, but we have faith that God will take care of us," they say. "We don't want to come right out and ask him for help." A woman who occasionally looks in on the old couple nods her head. "I'm praying for them," she says. "I'd like to ask God for their rent money and a bag of groceries, but he must know what they need better than I do. And if he knows, why would we have to ask?"

We live in a world that is full of material needs. At this moment I can think of a handicapped man who needs a job to restore his self-respect and sense of usefulness; a mother with a brain-damaged child who needs a means of transportation to get her daughter to the nearest special school; a Southeast Asian refugee family that needs housing, food, and a tutor to help them with their new language. And there are many more. Yet in so many of these instances we hear the same words: "I just can't ask God for material things."

I know exactly why these people hesitate, for I've been there. My mind takes me back through the years to the time when Louie was in seminary and our fingernails were often ragged from scraping the bottom of the barrel. We didn't feel comfortable then asking God for help in specific terms. We knew he was aware of our situation and we trusted him to help us, and we felt that was the end of the matter. It wasn't. God did help us, but along the way he brought us to a new understanding of what it means to ask for our daily bread.

Jesus himself told us to ask our Father for our daily bread, and yet, when it comes down to putting our needs into words, many of us falter. We feel selfish, greedy—yes, materialistic! —asking for such down-to-earth commodities as money, a place to live, a job, a car or access to dependable transportation, or training to make us more useful in the world. We don't want to bother God with such practical matters, so we keep these concerns to ourselves, reserving our prayers for things "more spiritual."

Yet there is that word *bread,* and what could be more down-to-earth than that? Surely, if Jesus meant for us to communicate with God only about spiritual matters, he would have used a different word. Bread is the simplest kind of food, the very staple of life from the beginning of recorded time. It has literally been the nutritional mainstay of civilization. And it is nourishment we need regularly, day by day, as Jesus also acknowledged by calling it "our *daily* bread."

Still—there are those questions about asking for material resources. I hear them often. Why, in the first place, do we have to ask for material resources at all? How should we ask? How long should we wait for an answer? Is it all right to ask again? And again? Suppose God says no? Can we ask for any material things we want or need? How can we be sure we aren't being selfish?

These were the questions that came to our minds when Louie and I began to explore petitionary prayer. We were in seminary, and had turned down a job with a regular paycheck so we would be free to do weekend deputation work for the school. Our only income was whatever the churches we visited might—or might not—give us at the end of each weekend, and since many of them were small, their gifts barely covered our transportation costs. But never mind, we were able to live frugally; we were doing what we wanted to do, and what we felt God wanted us to do—so we were happy.

Then one day we had to face the fact that we had hardly any food left. Strange, the things you remember—we had exactly one egg and one thirteen-ounce can of tomato juice, and no money to buy more. Our need was specific, and real—so, putting our questions aside, we decided to take our need to God.

I remember how uncomfortable we felt, kneeling and praying together for something as practical and unspiritual as our next meal. But we did it, believing that if God didn't approve of it, he would somehow let us know. "Lord, we're not complaining," we said, "but if we are doing what you want us to do, we need money for food to keep us going—and gasoline to get us to these churches. We don't need much, Lord, but we need it in a hurry!"

Later in the day, during a study break, Louie walked down

the hill to our mailbox and brought back a letter from a church we had visited months before. As he opened it and read—"Sorry to be late—thanks, and God bless!"—a check for forty dollars fell to the floor. Forty dollars! We couldn't have been more thrilled if it had been four hundred. For it wasn't just money, it was an answer to a specific asking prayer —and for us, a new understanding of what it meant to pray for our daily bread.

Several days later we received a letter from a good friend in East Germany, a fellow theological student we had met the previous summer when we were in a European work camp. Joachim was having a very hard time serving three small churches in his Communist-occupied homeland. The churches were quite far apart, and Joachim had no means of transportation. The government was making life especially hard for Christians, and it was critically important for Joachim to be able to continue to serve his congregations. "If only I could buy a motorcycle," he wrote in that letter. "I know that in your country, ministers have access to more money than we have here," he went on, "and that is why I am writing to you. Because you are my brother and sister, I'm asking you if you have an extra $250 you could send me." With our new freedom to ask for specific needs, Louie said, "Let's pray."

With a sense of adventure he said, "Lord, if one of the churches we visit soon could manage it, please let us have $250 for Joachim." It would have to be a fairly sizable church.

And it was. A few days later we received an invitation to visit a *very* large church in Texas. They were perfectly willing to send us plane fare, and they wanted us to work with different groups all weekend. We said yes immediately, and I began packing.

They were a warm and gracious congregation, and as we finished the last meeting we felt we had received more than we had given. On Sunday evening, as the host committee drove us to the airport, one of them handed Louie two envelopes and thanked us for coming on such short notice. *Two* envelopes! That was unusual!

As soon as the plane was in the air, Louie took the envelopes out of his pocket and opened them. In the first was a check for one hundred dollars, almost what we needed to keep us going for another month. (Those were the days!) "Lord thank you, thank you!"

But in the second envelope was another check—for $250—a spontaneous, generous act on the part of the church. Joachim would have his motorcycle, his three churches would have a pastor, and our joy was more than we could express! All the way home we sat, silent for the most part, letting our hearts speak the praise we felt.

I have even known God to see and answer our needs before the urge to ask has even registered on our minds. That's how much God sees and feels our need—"before they call to me, I will answer, and while they are still speaking I will listen" says Isaiah (65:24; NEB). And Jesus told us: "Your Father knows what your needs are before you ask him" (Matt. 6:8; NEB).

After we graduated from seminary, we spent two years in postgrad study in Scotland, where our first two sons were born. Postgrad study over, it was time for us to get to work. We took a freighter from Liverpool, across the Atlantic Ocean to Montreal, then motored with our family to New York and Washington, D.C., and finally boarded a plane for California. We were hot and tired from our long, long journey —and had exactly thirty-two dollars in our pocket. We decided not to worry—or even to pray—about our financial needs. They could wait until we reached the West Coast— tomorrow!

In those days there were fewer cross-country flights than today, and the planes were smaller. They also traveled more slowly and made more stops, so it was going to be a tedious journey—especially with one toddler and another baby in arms. We tried to be good scouts, but we couldn't help wishing we could afford to rest up in a hotel for a day. And oh! for a nice warm bath!

We stopped in Chicago, where the plane began filling up quickly. Louie and I held Danny and Tim in our laps and wondered where so many people were going to sit. There wasn't a single empty seat. Then a harried-looking airline representative came aboard and stood in the aisle, holding his hand up to get everyone's attention.

"I'm awfully sorry," he began, "but we've overbooked this flight, and we just have to ask some of you to get off." There were murmurs of protest and he held up his hand again.

"Look—we're *really* sorry," he said. "We'll do our best to make it up to anyone who will volunteer to get off and take another plane tomorrow. We'll put you up in a hotel for the night, all expenses paid, and we'll give each of you one hundred dollars."

Louie and I didn't even look at each other—we knew what the other was thinking. Our hands shot up as soon as we heard the offer. Within minutes we were off the plane, had two hundred-dollar checks in our hands, and were on our way to a good night's rest in a hotel. The next morning, refreshed and thankful, we continued on our way home, God's generous grubstake in Louie's pocket.

Now, I'm not saying it was God who overbooked that plane. He has better things to do, and he doesn't make mistakes. But when our needs are urgent, he can make the most amazing use of life's ordinary situations. As Leslie Weatherhead said, "What is not his will can be his instrument."

And so, during all the years of our marriage and our life together as a family, God has supplied our material needs—not our greeds, but everything we have really needed to live, serve, and share. From the furniture in our first home (which we called our "early marriage" furniture, much of which we are still using today)—with each piece coming to us in the most ingenious way—to all the countless needs that arise in the process of raising a family. Always, as we have brought these needs to God in prayer, he has answered with a most amazing day-by-day provision.

I'll never forget one such day long ago. It was summer in California, in the early days of the new church in Bel Air, and our refrigerator had just broken down. It was an old one that was in the house when we moved in, and it was beyond repair. We didn't have the money to buy a new one at that time, but for some reason it didn't worry us. A refrigerator seemed like a small thing compared to the provision we were experiencing on every side of us. If somehow we got a new one, fine; if we didn't, well, we would manage. The word *how* never occurred to us. But it occurred to the plumber who was fixing our pipes. He came into the kitchen, looking for a cold drink, and asked me, "Where's your refrigerator?"

I was making coffee for a morning meeting. "Oh," I said casually, "we don't have one just now." Actually it had broken down the day before.

"You don't have a refrigerator?" the plumber said, as if he hadn't heard me correctly. I shook my head. "Mrs. Evans," he said, "it's ninety degrees outside—how do you live without a refrigerator?"

He must have wondered at my lack of concern. "Well—we manage," I said. But of course, he had seen our four children, and he knew!

The plumber went home for lunch and when he returned he was driving his pickup truck, and in the back of it was a refrigerator. "It's not new," he said, "but it works well. We kept this extra one in our garage, for soda and things like that. We don't really need it—and we'd like you folks to have it."

It was a fine refrigerator and served us many years. But, best of all, the plumber and his family began coming to our Sunday services and became real friends in the Lord.

I don't mean to imply that God responds to all our prayers by sending the answer to us the same day in a pickup truck.

Most often his answer is in the form of *providing ways* for us
to increase our income for specific needs—but, to us, that is
no less an answer to prayer.

For instance, we have needed a great deal of extra financial
help during the college years. Our four children are close in
age, so we have had very heavy college expenses in a concen-
trated period of time. Yet, wonderfully, God has helped us see
two of our children through college, and the other two are following close behind. Now we are involved in graduate schools
—with one son working on a Ph.D.-M.D. program, another
son headed toward law, and our married daughter and young-
est son hoping to go into seminary. We feel that an education
is a valid resource our children need to prepare them for life
—for service and sharing—so we can ask with boldness for
this resource, believing it will ultimately honor God. And
how God has answered—and is continuing to answer—our
prayers! One of the boys works full-time, and it appears he
will be able to handle his graduate school costs himself.
Another son has received a full fellowship that will cover all
his tuition and expenses. Part-time jobs for the other children
have not only brought financial help, but provided them with
wonderful exposure to creative situations and opened doors
to growth. I have had opportunities to add to the family income through writing and, sometimes, speaking (though I'm
much more comfortable with writing than I am with speaking,
and I sometimes have to talk to the Lord about that!). Louie
has been asked to speak to groups and conferences, which
have been exceedingly generous, almost as though they knew
our special needs. And then, when we have done all we could
do, have walked through all the doors God has opened for us,
and there is still need, there is the "angel" who somehow appears at just the right time, that person who doesn't really
know our specific need, yet senses through prayer and the
work of the Holy Spirit that he or she has something God
wants him or her to pass on to us. That is a humbling time for

me—but I am learning to be faithful in accepting such a gift, just as the "angel unaware" was seeking to be faithful in the giving.

Again, I want to share something from *George Mueller, Man of Faith,* for I feel close to George Muller's concept of asking for specific needs, not from any selfish motive to glut myself on more and more things, but in order to be free to serve: "I first began to allow God to deal with me . . . and set out fifty years ago simply relying on Him for myself, family, taxes, traveling expenses, and every other need," he wrote. "I've lacked nothing . . . nothing!"

And yet, when Mr. Muller was asked if he ever thought of requesting anything above and beyond straightforward needs, he paused, frowned, and reached into his coat pocket for a small change purse containing only a few coins. "All I am possessed of is in that purse," he said simply. I think it never occurred to him to want more. Yet he could pray boldly for every personal and family need, for every material resource for life, for service and for sharing. He asked for buildings to house his orphans, food to help them grow into healthy, strong adults, and clothing to keep them warm and present- able. He was never shy when it came to asking for—and ex- pecting to receive—anything that could bear fruit for God. And neither should we be!

# Chapter 11

## *Lord, Help Me to Feel*

Just as we can ask God for our spiritual and material needs, we can ask him to supply our emotional needs, which, when met, enable us to serve God better in this world.

Martin Luther's words, "our daily bread includes everything needed for this life," even "true friends and neighbors," reminds me of a Sunday morning six years ago. Our family had moved from one coast to the other a few weeks earlier, and I was now far from where I had grown up, married, and raised our children. We were "easterners" now, living in Washington, D.C., where Louie had accepted a new call.

I had fallen in love with Washington and its great mixture of people, and we had been warmly welcomed by our new congregation. I was eager to plunge into the work that was waiting to be done in this big, capital-city congregation and the world around it. But even though my mind was challenged and stimulated to begin, my heart seemed to lag behind, looking back wistfully and longing for the people we had left in California.

Frankly, I felt a little ashamed of myself. After meeting so many cordial people in Washington, how could I feel lonely? I told myself to stop being childish and threw myself into the ongoing round of luncheons, neighborhood coffees, and receptions designed to help welcome me into my new environment. But the longing continued. As one warm hand after another grasped mine on reception lines, I wanted to hold on to each one a little longer. I wanted more than a smile, a greeting, and good wishes. Each new person went on his or her way so quickly! We were all so busy, there seemed to be no room in our lives for deep relationships.

In California I had known friendships that were years in the making. I had deep covenant relationships with people who had truly shared my life by allowing me to share theirs. Together we had been through joys and crises, we had laughed and cried together, and there was no problem we couldn't pray about with one another.

It was that kind of relationship I was longing for. I needed a person . . . not someone to keep me company or to go places with, but someone to share a supportive relationship. Yes, I had my husband, and how I thanked God for Louie! My first and most meaningful human covenant is with him. I had my children, and they were great—but they had their own lives, and their teenage need was to have me *not* need them. Although I am first and always a wife and mother, I am also a person—a "people person"—and I have a need for real friends both within and without the family circle.

As I sat in church that morning six years ago, the confusion I had been feeling began to clear, and just as we finished singing a hymn, I understood that I was not being childish. I had a legitimate human need for an emotional resource that would enable me to serve God better in this new place. So right then and there, I sat down and prayed.

"Lord," I remember thinking to God, "I need a friend. I know you have work for me to do, and you know how much I want to do it, but I need a person, Lord. I don't know who— but someone to make room in her life for me . . . and someone who needs me in her life as well. Someone I can pray with —and I want *you* to pick her out. I ask this in the name of your Son, Jesus, who also had the need for close relationships." (I was thinking, at that moment, of the way Jesus loved his disciples, also of the way he went back, and back again, to a certain home in the town of Bethany, whenever he was in the area, to see his dear friends Lazarus, Mary, and Martha. Although these three friends were not among his twelve disciples, he confided in them, lovingly sharing with them his thoughts and his very life, because, as the Bible describes them, they were very sensitive to Jesus' special emotional needs.) I felt better having prayed.

Several Sundays later, in church, I sat down behind a woman I recognized. I had been at a luncheon with her, and she had shaken my hand in *several* receiving lines. At the close of the service, she turned around and, leaning toward me, whispered, "What do you do on Thursday mornings?"

"Nothing I can't change!" I answered eagerly.

"I have the strongest feeling we should be together on a regular basis," she said. "Does that mean anything to you?"

"Yes!" I said, blinking back my tears.

Her name was Mary Jane, and as we began meeting on Thursday mornings simply to be together and to pray, I felt a resource I deeply needed returning to my life. We were not just acquaintances—we became part of each other's lives. We helped each other discover our strengths and leaned on each other in our weaknesses, and before long we were reaching out to other women with the same longing for a supportive covenant relationship that simply said, "I love you," without attaching any conditions. Nor was it in any way exclusive, for out of the spiritual nurture of that group each one of us felt strengthened to reach out to others—and to increase our involvement in our city and in our world.

Now, when I look back to that Sunday morning in church, I offer another prayer of thanks to God: for awakening me to the fact that I wasn't being greedy or selfish—or childish—in wanting that kind of relationship. We *need* supportive people in our lives. God made us to live *interdependently*—it is the way we serve him best—and people are a resource we can ask him to supply. This is part of our daily bread.

Another emotional resource we need, and can ask for, is that of a deep inner security that comes from knowing God. This is a security that will allow us to take risks in life, for he will not always answer our prayers according to our definition of "success." Sometimes our failure can be of greater use to him.

For Jesus, the cross appeared to be the abrupt end of a ministry that once seemed full of promise. Yet that same cross —an apparent failure—became our salvation. The scattering of the disciples by their Roman persecutors seemed certain to obliterate any hope that the news of a Redeemer might persist. But by means of that scattering—that "failure"—Christianity spread throughout the world.

". . . I have been longing for many years to visit you on my way to Spain; for I hope to see you as I travel through [Rome], and to be sent there with your support after having enjoyed your company for a while" (Rom. 15:24; NEB), Paul wrote to the Christians in Rome. But he never reached Spain. Instead, his journey took him to a Roman prison, and death.

Did Paul fail in what he was trying to do? So it might have seemed, but from his prison cell he wrote, "Friends, I want you to understand that the work of the Gospel has been helped on, rather than hindered, by this business of mine. My imprisonment in Christ's cause has become common knowledge to all at headquarters here [the imperial guard], and indeed among the public at large; and it has given confidence to most of our fellow-Christians to speak the word of God fearlessly and with extraordinary courage" (Phil. 1:12–14; NEB). Paul saw his apparent failure used as an instrument of God, and he rejoiced. And while we have no idea what might have come of his journey to Spain, we do know what an influence Paul's prison letters have been on the lives of all Christians. His way of viewing the situation had to come from a deep, unthreatened emotional security in knowing God, a security that enabled him to assure us: ". . . I know who it is in whom I have trusted, and am confident of his power to keep safe what he has put into my charge, until the great Day" (2 Tim. 1:12; NEB).

When we ask God to use us, it is perfectly all right for us to offer him our own plans of action, but we must realize that our plans are subject to change. We can't possibly see the "big picture" the way God can, and he may have something else on his agenda for our lives. We need to be ready to pray the "nevertheless" prayer, having the deep-down certainty that all things work together for good for "those who love God and are called according to his purpose" (Rom. 8:28; NEB).

It may take us a long time to understand how God can use seeming failure to his advantage, and sometimes, when we ask God for our daily bread, we may find its taste bitter and its substance hard to digest. We may ask for the emotional resource of support on an issue close to our heart and be given the strength instead to take a lonely stand. God may ask us to endure ridicule, anger, and loneliness—and give us the strength to do it. And in the eyes of others we may indeed seem to fail in serving him. Never mind. God sees many more things than we do, and even in our worst failure for his sake there can be great good.

Some years ago, when Senator Mark Hatfield first began to speak out against U.S. involvement in Vietnam, he was very much alone. So fierce were the hostilities he provoked that some thought he was jeopardizing his political career—he would never be elected to office again, some people were saying. Even some of his fellow Christians responded in wrath, one letter beginning with the salutation: "Dear former brother in Christ. . . ." But all during that time, Senator Hatfield's concern was not with his political future, it was with speaking out on something he believed was right, even if it wasn't popular. It was a hard time in his life—a failure, some people called it. But it was the kind of failure God could use, and he did.

The Bible is full of stories about people asking for, and receiving, the emotional resources they needed to get God's job done. The young shepherd boy David faced the giant of the Philistine army—alone. Goliath roared his insults daily at the army of Israel, laughing at both them and their God. David refused armor and swords when he went to meet the giant, taking only his slingshot and choosing five smooth stones for ammunition. But David went trusting in the Lord's strength. He said to the giant, "You have come against me with sword and spear and dagger, but I have come against you in the name of the Lord of Hosts, the God of the army of Israel which you have defied. The Lord will put you into my power this day" (1 Sam. 17:45–46; NEB). Like David, we can seek strength from the Lord our God to meet the giants we have to face.

One emotional resource I have come to depend upon God to supply, over and over again, is the sense of quietness and confident certainty that he is in control—of my life, of the lives of my family and friends, and of history. "Thou dost keep in peace men of constant mind, in peace because they trust in thee. Trust in the Lord for ever; for the Lord himself is an everlasting rock" (Isa. 26:3–4; NEB). "Come back, keep peace, and you will be safe; in stillness and in staying quiet, there lies your strength" (Isa. 30:15; NEB). Those are words I have come to love as through the years the Lord has daily met the emotional need of quietness and confidence no other person or material thing could ever provide.

There are other emotional resources God is waiting to provide for us day by day. For instance, each of us has a need to be healed of past emotional scars, and God urges us to stop hugging these hurts, so he can restore our spirits and add inner strength to our lives. But God will not take away every painful or difficult situation from our lives. In Isaiah 41:10–13 he says: "Fear not . . . I am with you; do not look around you in terror and be dismayed, for I am your God. I will strengthen and harden you [to difficulties] . . . for I, the Lord your God, hold your right hand . . ." (Amplified). His way is not necessarily to remove our difficulties, but to give us the inner resources we need to meet those difficulties through the strengthening of our spirit. If we never experienced difficulties, we couldn't grow out of our childish thoughts and expectations. But, remaining in childlike dependency upon a loving, heavenly Father, who will guide us through the difficulties, we grow into men and women who are like Christ. What a resource for life!

Sorrow is one of the greatest emotional difficulties we will have to face in life—and often many times. When we mourn over the loss of people we love, and when death seems to be an irrevocable loss—and in this life, it is—we will have to find the emotional resources we need to meet these losses. If we can allow the available resources—even those built into the process of natural, human grief—to minister to us, we can be healed of the deep wounds that death creates, and we will also be able to minister to others. For us and for those around us, the way we handle our deepest griefs can mean the difference between sorrow and tragedy.

In Galatians 6:2 we read, "Help one another to carry these heavy loads" (NEB), and in Psalm 55:22, "Commit your fortunes to the Lord, and he will sustain you" (NEB). Although these passages seem to be contradictory, they really aren't. When we allow another trusted person to share our suffering, our problems, and our deep human needs, we are actually making it possible for God to give us strength through the care and concern of others. Still, there are some sorrows in life that only God can help us to endure, for no one else can really know or share in the deepest heart pains—or joys—of another human being.

God wants us to ask for the healing of our sorrows; he does not want them to cripple us for life. By his Son's wounds we can be healed, and his Son was wounded unto death. God also wants us to understand that this kind of petitionary prayer requires waiting, resting, and trusting. Our weeping may last for a night—perhaps a very long night, or even a season of life—but if we wait patiently, there will surely be joy in the morning (Ps. 30:5). "Don't be impatient," the Psalmist tells us. "Wait for the Lord; be strong, take courage, and wait for the Lord" (Ps. 27:14; NEB).

Our sorrow must run its entire course in order to be healed. As each wave of grief flows in upon us, like the tides of the sea, sometimes overwhelming us, we must not fight them, but must, instead, give in to them as part of the healing process. Each wave has its Godly purpose.

I have been with many friends as they mourned the death of one they loved. And I have mourned, too, most recently after the death of my mother. I have felt the waves of sorrow wash over my heart, and I have been healed by their hidden strength.

At first, when a loved one dies, we cannot believe we are going to be separated from the person we love and need. It simply doesn't seem possible, and we try to push the fact from our mind. We may think we are having a bad dream and will soon wake up to find it never happened. But eventually we have no choice but to accept both the death and the loss. We are helpless to do anything about it.

Next comes the numbing shock, which may be a bit of an anesthetic from God. The numbness gets us through the necessary duties and details that accompany death in our world. But everything seems dull and out of focus. We seem unable to feel—anything.

And then, sometimes much later, comes a wave of awareness on a deeper level as the shock subsides. We begin to *feel* again, and we are almost grateful, even though our first feeling is one of pain and loneliness. The pain increases as we realize we will never again, in our life on this earth, see the person who died. We will never be quite the same without him or her, and we ache inside. But remembering that the person we love is actually beginning a new and wonderful spiritual existence, closer to our Lord, makes the ache more bearable.

Along with each wave of grief we experience there is a

different emotion, and if we are to be healed completely we must not try to cut ourselves off from these feelings, however difficult and painful they may be. God works through them to restore us to health.

Some of us will feel anger as we become aware of death. We may rage at being left here alone. Or, like a young man I know whose father died at an early age, we may feel anger at a loved one for not taking better care of his or her health. We may be angry with death itself, which is a natural expression of human helplessness in the face of such a terrible finality to physical existence.

We may feel some guilt. In fact, guilt is almost impossible to avoid. Why, we may wonder, did the loved one die—why did he or she "fail"—while we are still "successfully" alive? And even in the best relationships, some needed things are always left undone, some needed words unsaid. Yes, the wave of guilt is always distressing, but it must be met.

Sometimes we will be overcome by waves of depression, even despair. A psychologist friend describes this sensation as a "breathlessness—a feeling that vitality and life are just beyond our grasp" (Myron Madden, *Raise the Dead!*). We feel as if our loved one has been torn from the roots of our lives, and we are painfully conscious of the void that is left.

To make matters worse for us, we live in a world where there is no room for grief, no place where we can freely shed our tears. Perhaps the ancient concept of the professional mourner was not without merit, for when someone else mourns out loud, without shame or apology, the bereaved feel free to express their grief. But in our modern world there seems to be no place where we can cry out loud. As Myron Madden said, the "walls are too thin" and "our offices too crowded" for a healthy expression of sorrow. In his own grief, the author discovered that the only place where he could cry out loud was in his car, with the windows rolled up, while driving at night. And when I read that, I felt a throb of familiarity.

Like so many other mourners, I had fought and finally accepted the awareness that my mother had died. But I felt checked in an emotional holding pattern as I went through her things and made the arrangements for her memorial service. I knew there were tears inside me—indeed they fell easily and often—but I couldn't allow myself to release the flood I sensed was waiting to break over me because my stepfather was devastated by grief, and I felt I couldn't add my burden to his at such a time. So I went through those days almost "breathless," knowing a time of reckoning would come.

Then, later in the week after the memorial service, I had to go on an errand and I chose to go alone. It was dark as I was returning home, and the ocean was behind me. Suddenly I knew why I didn't want anyone to accompany me—I needed to be alone. The pain inside me begged for release. Now. I rolled up the windows and let the sobs come as hard as they would. I felt a terrible agony convulse my body. The hard, cold fact was that my mother's physical presence was gone from my life. I would never see her face, or hear her voice, or read her words in the familiar slant of her writing in letters I always loved to receive. I was so lonely for her. But my face was wet with tears, and I did feel—and I thanked God for it. The healing had begun. The agony of mourning helped me get to the core of my pain. I couldn't walk away from it. I couldn't postpone it. The waves had to wash over me, every one of them, before they could subside.

Other people can comfort and console us in our grief. They can be part of the healing, but only after all the waves of mourning have washed through our lives. Comfort can come only after we can accept death as a reality in life, and only as Jesus brings us to the realization that physical death is not the end of our life. Oh no—there is much more life to come! The Indian poet Rabindranath Tagore explains, "Death is not the extinguishing of the light—it is the putting out of the lamp because the dawn has come." The "morning star" that "rises to illuminate our minds" that Peter talks about (2 Pet. 1:19;

NEB) is the very life of Jesus Christ—which we will share in forever!

Our life with God only begins here on earth, and it doesn't end with our death. It goes on and on, expanding and extending. We will be given new, heavenly bodies in that new experience of more life in Christ. Someday we, too, will exist in a closer relationship with him after we have passed through the entryway of our own physical death. But for now we must wait for the healing he alone can bring us in our loneliness and sorrow. We must wait for the gift of restoration—emotional healing—he has promised to give us, if only we will ask him for it as part of our bread for life.

My eye once caught a quotation in a popular magazine, and I have never forgotten it. It fits here: "God will mend a broken heart . . . if you give him all the pieces."

## Chapter 12

## Lord, Heal Me

Health and strength for our bodies are a valid portion of our daily bread. As children of a loving, heavenly Father, we are urged to ask for this part of the loaf by the example we see in the life of our Lord.

Much of Jesus' ministry on earth was involved with the healing of men, women, and children who were physically, mentally, or spiritually afflicted. Wherever he went, people came to him believing that he could heal their illnesses, and he was always moved with compassion by their suffering. Surely God's perfect will for us is wholeness—if not, then Jesus was a great violator of God's will.

It is interesting to note that the Greek word for *holy*—which is a word describing both Jesus and his Father—has the meaning "health, healthy, hale, hearty, and whole" about it. Paul tells us in no uncertain terms that God created us to be whole human beings—"May God himself, the God of peace, make you holy in every part, and keep you sound in spirit, soul, and body, without fault. . . . He who calls you is to be trusted; he will do it" (1 Thess. 5:23–24; NEB). He wants us to "enjoy good health, . . . that all may go well with you, as . . . it goes well with your soul" (3 John 2; NEB), because health and strength are so interrelated that one can be infected by the illness—or healed by the recovery—of the other. The writer of the Proverbs says, "A merry heart doeth good like a medicine" (17:22; KJV), and it can work the other way, too: the health and vibrancy of a spirit can help a dying physical body do seemingly superhuman feats and can bring a lovely grace even to a crippled form.

Even before we were in the ministry "officially," my husband and I had experiences that confirmed our belief that God was concerned with the physical well-being of his people. We were in Edinburgh, Scotland, and Louie was finishing two years of postgraduate work in New Testament studies. We found a close relationship among the students at New College, and after dinner one particular evening we sat around the fire with Chuck, a fellow student, warming our feet and drinking mugs of steaming tea. Chuck told us of a married fellow American student who had just been told by doctors at the Royal Infirmary that he was gravely ill. The X rays and tests had revealed a fast-growing malignant tumor, and the Scottish doctors advised him and his wife to go home immediately. The three of us prayed together around the fire for our sick friend's healing, but somehow that did not seem to be enough. We felt the Spirit saying to us, "Go to him and in faith pray and anoint him with oil." Now, this was something none of us had ever done—and even the thought of doing it seemed "far out" and frightening. However, in obedience, we went to our sick friend, and with his eager consent, Louie and Chuck offered prayers for his healing and anointed him with olive oil taken from my kitchen cupboard. Almost immediately our friend and his wife left for the United States, and for years we had no word of what happened after that night. Then, one day much later, we saw him—tall and strong and healthy— energetically involved in a conference we were attending. After we hugged one another, overjoyed at being together again, he told us the story we were waiting to hear. He and his wife had taken the X rays and medical report and flown home to the United States to be under the care of his own doctor, and be close to his family, for the diagnosis was grave indeed

—"possibly as little as six weeks." As soon as it could be arranged, his doctor took more X rays to check on the growth of the tumor, and to his astonishment there was no trace of it. The tumor was absolutely gone—our friend was healed. He knew it, the doctor knew it, and God was given all the thanks and praise.

Since hearing this account from our friend, Louie and I have become friends of the man who was pastor to him and his family during the crisis of that illness. He saw both sets of X rays, and could only say to us, "It was a miracle—that's all —a miracle."

We thank God for this early experience of asking for, and receiving, a complete physical healing, not only because it meant life for someone we care about, and enabled him to minister in health and strength for twenty-five years since that time, but also for the lesson it held for us. Since that time the passage from James 5:14–15—"Is one of you ill? He should send for the elders of the congregation to pray over him and anoint him with oil in the name of the Lord. The prayer offered in faith will save the sick man, the Lord will raise him from his bed, and any sins he may have committed will be forgiven" (NEB)—has been a part of our lives and our work. We have prayed, and seen God heal—within our family, among our friends, and within the three congregations we have served.

Health for the body is often the daily bread we need, and there have been many powerful examples of its provision through the ages. Martin Luther wrote: "No one believes how strong and mighty prayer is and how much it can do except he whom experience has taught, and who has tried it." He then went on to describe his own healing, and the healing his wife, Katherina, experienced as she "lay in danger of death." More recently, Dr. E. Stanley Jones during his life was absolutely certain that his health was restored through the power of petitionary prayer, and he is only one of many who have made that claim. A woman who was close to death during the criti-

cal period following open-heart surgery said she could actually feel her body rally as her family and friends prayed for
healing night and day.

Yes, we believe in asking for health and healing, and we
have seen God answer such prayers, many times! But we have
also seen that there is no simple answer to every such request.
God is in control, and sometimes in his infinite love and wisdom he decides that, besides physical health and strength,
there are other very important things he wants us, our friends,
or our loved ones to have. Beautiful, talented Joni Eareckson
struggled for months to get a "healed" answer from God. She
had been paralyzed from the shoulders down in a diving accident, and has to win through years of suffering—and asking
—and questioning—and receiving the answers God intended
for her. But through her struggling she has brought strength
to many, many people. In the prayer for physical resources, as
in any of the asking prayers, we must be prepared to pray the
"nevertheless" prayer, for all of the circumstances of our lives
are under his control.

While it is perfectly right for us to ask God for healing, we
must not simply ignore the other provisions for good health
that he has already given us. Each day, many new discoveries
in the field of medicine make it possible for us to live
healthier, longer lives, and I think we are meant to receive
this resource, thankfully. We also must take responsibility for
our own health. We cannot ignore the wisdom of getting the
proper amount of rest, nutritious food, exercise, and relaxation, and expect God to exempt us from the consequences of
our deliberate disobedience. Even when we do fall ill, however, God can use that illness to our advantage if we will
allow him.

For the past several years, Louie and I have realized that
our lives were going too fast. There was always so much that
"had to be done," and the days we put aside for rest and
relaxation kept getting gobbled up by emergencies. We were
caught in "the tyranny of the urgent" and were missing an im-

portant resource for both of us—rest and our time alone together. But the work was there, and we kept saying that someday soon we would get away for those days of rest. Finally,
last spring, right after Easter, we did—but it was too late. By
the time we arrived at the little mountain cabin we had rented,
Louie was very yellow . . . and very ill. After blood tests, a
doctor diagnosed his symptoms as acute viral hepatitis, and
told him he probably would have been able to resist it if he
hadn't been so exhausted.

Hepatitis is a very debilitating illness, and the recovery time
is long, requiring rest, most of it in bed. Louie had no choice
but to delegate much of his work to others, who were eager
to help, and I canceled all those appointments that had once
seemed so necessary.

We followed our doctor's orders scrupulously, but we knew
God was also helping in the healing process. We had some les-
sons to learn, for though we had no doubt God could restore
Louie's body to health, we knew the illness would surely recur
if he didn't slow down the pace of his life. Changing that pattern is where the greatest amount of healing was needed. How
can a person who is a born activist do all he wants to do and
still stay healthy? It was a question that required God's answer.

The answer came, but in a remarkably subtle, surprising
manner. It came during the long hours of convalescence when
we rediscovered the strength we had in Christ, the strength
that comes from quietness with him, as we had unhurried
trysts with him and with each other. The answer came as we
listened to music, and tapes of sermons, and began reading
the pile of books that had waited so long to be opened. The
answer came as we saw that the world kept on spinning without us, and that there were many talented lay people, men and
women, ready and willing to help with the work; and that
some of the awesome work load we felt was so urgent was
simply unnecessary. We learned that there were more important ways for us to serve the Lord than in running from one

meeting to another without asking ourselves whether our running was the wisest use of our time. We know better than to fool ourselves into thinking that we will never again have to fight the battle of busyness—but we did take a big step in the direction of God's pacing for our lives, where less, done his way, can really be more.

By the time Louie recovered his physical strength, he also felt healing in this other area of his life. And now there is no question in our minds: God has used this physical illness as a time of deep blessing for us both, to get us more closely in touch with his desires for us.

George Buttrick raises another issue in his wonderful little book on prayer. What does it mean when our prayers for healing appear to go unanswered? He writes: "Why deny these facts? It is doubtful if people would ever fall sick and die if all prayers were answered." He brings us to that haunting passage in Ecclesiastes and we remember that there is a time to be born, a time to live, and a time to die (3:2)—and no matter how urgently we pray, we know God will not set aside his time for our life and death.

Some of our prayers for healing will not be answered in the way we ask: often we will have to face physical separation from—even the loss of—friends and family through death. When this happens, and it becomes apparent that death is God's will for a person, then we cannot honestly pray for healing and at the same time be serving his will. Then, painful though it will be, we must pray the prayer of relinquishment, and give the one we love to God for his ultimate healing.

It is not easy to loosen our grip on the physical life of the person we are losing, however temporarily. It is an agony—especially when the person is someone very close to us—to accept the realization that we will never see that one again on this earth. As we try to bow our head to pray the prayer of relinquishment our neck may stiffen—and we may find we cannot do it in our own strength. That is when we ourselves need a special kind of healing, and we must not hesitate to ask God for it.

*But*—while it is still time to live and serve and share, we should not hesitate to pray with faith and boldness for healing and health. For it is never selfish when we use our health as a resource to serve God and his children in this world.

# PART IV

## THE IMPERATIVE TO SHARE

# Chapter 13

## The Need to Share

Our earth seen from miles out in space looks like a lovely shining green and blue ball, the edges of the continents familiar to us who have studied maps since we were children in school. Every day we realize with new poignancy that our earth *is* a relatively small global community. Nations as well as individuals are and must be interdependent. The discoveries for good as well as the inhuman tragedies that affect one *do* affect all the others, immediately or eventually, and there will be no reversal of this fact now until the end of time. From this time forward all the people of the world will have to acknowledge the effect of their words and actions on every other person. Therefore, the question is no longer *if* I will touch another human being but, rather, *because I must* affect other persons, *how* shall I do so?

We are faced today with the growing awareness of America's relative wealth—its abundance of material resources—in a world where many nations struggle to feed all their population. America has been called the breadbasket of the world, for its policy of giving billions of dollars' worth of foodstuffs—grain, rice, and corn—to nations that are needy, and in the past has often simply written off the cost. This generosity would not be possible without, first, the presence of a surplus of foodstuffs produced, and second, the willingness of individuals in our nation to share our resources. Yet, for all the items on the credit side, we need to accept the fact that among the seventeen most-developed nations, we are thirteenth in terms of our giving. Every day our television sets bring us pictures of malnourished orphans—homeless, rejected, desolate boat people—war-torn men, women, and children, uprooted in their own land, existing in a living death. Even within our own nation, despite its overall affluence, there are individuals whose lives are not brightened today by the prospect of a tomorrow—because one more day will only be a repetition of today's squalor and despair.

These vivid pictures of human misery alongside the experience of our material blessings makes me increasingly uncomfortable in my own comfort—and I am asking the question "What can I do to help?" with greater determination and impatience. And yet I know the helplessness in that very question.

Some years ago, when the PBS network was filming the documentary *World Hunger—Who Will Survive?*, narrator Bill Moyers related how one of his friends, upon hearing of the film, exclaimed, "Bloated bodies! Bloated bodies! Don't show us any more bloated bodies. I know they are there, but what can I do about it?"

There is a kind of helplessness in realizing that statistics on world hunger indicate that 2 out of every 10 people (600 to 800 million) are malnourished, while 40 to 50 million people are in danger of death from starvation. There is a kind of helplessness in realizing that, with less than 6 percent of the world's population, the United States uses about one third of the world's physical resources in production and well over one third of the world's present energy resources. There is a helplessness in realizing that most of the world's recoverable oil will have been used by the middle of the next century, and we may be doing great harm to the ecological balance of the "little" world we share by our unchecked use of fuels and chemicals today. And that's only on the "material resources" ledger. An equal helplessness appears when I think of the other needs in the world today: emotional, spiritual, physical, and the need for persons to experience wholeness and health. So many people I know are hungry for God—for meaning in their lives —for worthwhile relationships with others. Even the resource of time is a very scarce commodity today, and we often fail to share our time even with those who should be closest to us, or those who need our attention the most. The need for sharing resources is everywhere, and on every level.

We live in a world of inequality. There are God-created inequalities among individuals—those differing talents, abilities, and preferences for tasks that make us interdependent. There are personality inequalities—as one person is more sensitive to emotional needs than another, or can encourage people with a lightness of spirit. There are financial inequalities—as changing jobs or opportunities or needs bring our financial status up or down. It seems that inequality is built into the very fabric of life.

But there is one way in which all people are equal: each person who has ever lived upon the earth—or live now, or will live in the future—is loved by God the Father—loved so much that the Father sent his only beloved Son to take the penalty of our sin upon himself, and through his death to bring us life. When the Bible says that God created all things through his Word, and then that the Word became flesh, and lived among us, showing us how to live in relationship with God, it is declaring again and again that God considers our global community worthwhile—so worthwhile that he should visit it himself. Each human being has equal worthiness in the eyes of God and receives life ultimately from him.

When we become children of the heavenly Father through receiving Jesus, and becoming his disciples, we gain many brothers and sisters, namely, all the people on earth! God loves them all, equally, and he is going to love them through us. Our Catholic friends have a keen understanding of this truth when they say that we are Christ's arms, legs, hands, and mouths in this world.

I love the story dear Corrie ten Boom tells in *Plenty for Everyone:* "I once read a legend about Christ's return to heaven, when He had finished His work in this world. As He arrived at the shore of heaven the angels ran to meet Him, eagerly questioning Him about His work on earth among men.

" 'Did you complete your work of redemption?'

" 'Yes, it is finished.'

" 'Who will make it known?'

" 'I have told Peter, John, Philip, and all who are my disciples.'

" 'And what if they fail?'

" 'I have no other plan, and they will not fail.' "

Corrie goes on to remind us that Jesus can entrust to our care the important task of taking the Gospel to the lost all over the world because he has given us everything necessary for the job: we have the Holy Spirit for power (Acts 1:8), and the boundless resources of Christ himself. "And it is in God's power to provide you richly with every good gift; thus you will have ample means in yourselves to meet each and every situation, with enough and to spare for every good cause" (2 Cor. 9:8; NEB).

The Lord, while he was among us, told us how he would know his true followers. In Matthew (25:31–46) we read that those who have the Father's blessing will feed the hungry, give the thirsty drink, take the stranger into their homes, clothe the naked, help the ill, and visit those in prison. In his parable, Jesus assures us that anything we do for one of his brothers, however humble, we do for him.

So we have the Lord's will clearly before us: Jesus told us to share our daily resources with those who do not have enough to meet their needs. But, in order to share, we must first have something *to* share. Foreseeing that, Jesus taught us how to view our resources, whether they be spiritual, material, emotional, or physical. He said we are to be stewards of these resources. It is as if God is lending us certain talents to develop while we are here, to produce different kinds of wealth—not only goods, services, and money, but health and good attitudes!—and to use that wealth to bless others.

The ability to meet our own needs is given by God. The ability to share freely with others in their need is also given by God. When we die, we will not take our accumulated things with us, but while we are on this earth we have the opportunity to serve the Lord—and build his Kingdom—by helping others meet their needs. By sharing, we allow the love and power of God to flow through us.

Still, in spite of the need we see, the command we hear, and the blessing we want to share, there are some who question sharing for one reason or another. Some are simply overwhelmed by the need. Recently, in our congregation, when a special hunger offering was taken for Cambodian relief, a visitor worshiping with us objected, saying, "Oh, it's just too overwhelming—nothing we do can make a difference, really." But the response of the congregation made it clear that the great majority did not share that view, and their generosity indicated that they welcomed an opportunity to do something—*anything*—to help.

Not all the glaring need for material resources comes from devastation of war. "You have the poor among you always," said Jesus, when one of his disciples protested about an extravagant display of love by a woman who poured a costly oil on his head (Matt. 26:6–13; NEB). Jesus seems to acknowledge over and over that poverty does exist, and that the poor have something very important to teach us. Although "poverty" and "wealth" can be relative terms, there is a level of poverty that marks those who live in it constantly with a despair of spirit. The writer of the Proverbs prays, "Two things I ask of thee; do not withhold them from me before I die. Put fraud and lying far from me; give me neither poverty nor wealth, provide me only with the food I need. If I have too much, I shall deny thee and say, 'Who is the Lord?' If I am reduced to poverty, I shall steal and blacken the name of my God" (Prov. 30:7–9; NEB).

I was troubled recently to read these words of Henry Ward Beecher, who, I understand, reflected an attitude toward poverty apparently not uncommon in his time: "No man in this land suffers from poverty unless it be more than his fault—unless it be his sin. . . . There is enough and to spare thrice over: and if men have not enough, it is owing to the worst of provident care, and foresight, and industry, and frugality, and wise saving. This is the general truth." He seems to be saying that the poor are lazy, extravagant, and careless, and that they bring their poverty upon themselves. He appears to view poverty as a result of sin and therefore undeserving of our help.

But just as wealth can be inherited and does not necessarily reflect the merit of those who now possess it, so can poverty—and all the dehumanizing conditions that go with it—be passed on, from father to son and mother to daughter. Although it may be true that some laziness causes some poverty, so can some dishonest dealings cause wealth, so we can't guess at a person's worth by looking at his or her life-style. Our value can't be determined by how much we do—or don't —have but by how much we share, and by how effective we are as stewards of the wealth God has entrusted to us.

In the Bible we find the harshest judgment reserved for the "rich"—in any of life's resources—who have no regard for the "poor." Even at the very founding of the nation of Israel we sense the spirit Jesus was later to express throughout his parables and cautions: "When one of your fellow-countrymen in any of your settlements in the land which the Lord your God is giving you becomes poor, do not be hard-hearted or close-fisted with your countryman in his need. Be open-handed towards him and lend him on pledge as much as he needs. See that you do not harbour iniquitous thoughts when you find that the seventh year, the year of remission, is near, and look askance at your needy countryman and give him nothing. If you do, he will appeal to the Lord against you, and you will be found guilty of sin. Give freely to him and do not begrudge him your bounty, because it is for this very bounty that the Lord your God will bless you in everything that you do or undertake. The poor will always be with you in the land, and for that reason I command you to be open-handed with your countrymen, both poor and distressed, in your own land" (Deut. 15:7-11; NEB).

I think it is interesting that the instruction applies to both "poor and distressed." We know people who have large bank accounts yet whose hearts are ragged and shabby because they are lonely and cold in their "wealth." And we know others who have known the extravagance of giving—even when they had literally pennies left in their own pockets—and felt very wealthy doing it! The needy are not only the materially poor, but also the emotionally distressed, the spiritually hungry, the physically weak. Never mind if we have only a bit of bread and fish left over from our daily provision from God —it is meant to be shared with our needy brothers and sisters. God didn't give us more than we could use in order to stack it up all around us! He intends our joy to be *full*, and wants us to experience the very thrill he must feel day by day as he shares his abundant cupboard with us.

Paul wrote to the Corinthians, "Scripture says of such a man: 'He has lavished his gifts on the needy, his benevolence stands fast for ever.' Now he who provides seed for sowing and bread for food will provide the seed for you to sow; he will multiply it and swell the harvest of your benevolence, and you will always be rich enough to be generous" (2 Cor. 9:9-11; NEB). God intends us to experience generosity! Being children of the heavenly Father, that is one of our responsibilities!

When the King of kings visited the earth he had created, he was born to very poor parents. Wealthy kings from the East visited him while he was still an infant, but he was born in a stable. And the glory of heaven's angels appeared, not to the Roman or Jewish hierarchy, but to shepherds, simple hired men who cared for, but did not own, the sheep in the fields.

It is absurd to equate poverty with sin. Poverty is a condition, a fact of life—but a fact that provides the framework for our service. And there is no question that from his manger birth on through all the days of his life, Jesus identified with the poor. Can we really follow him and not share that concern? Can we come to him at all, if we don't see our own poverty?

In all truth, we are the poor helping the poor—and I know no better example than Mother Teresa of Calcutta, India. In 1937, when this remarkable woman was teaching at the Loreto convent school in Calcutta, six years after she had answered God's call to become a nun, she went into one of the worst, most depressed sections of the city for the first time. People who have seen slums in all parts of the world say that those in Calcutta are miserable beyond belief, and anyone who has no business there is usually happy to stay away from them. But Mother Teresa had a different reaction: she felt as if she belonged there . . . that God was calling her a second time.

It was not an easy call to answer, as we learn from her own words describing her feelings about leaving the convent:

"Our Lord wants me to be a free nun, covered with the poverty of the Cross. But today I learned a great lesson. The poverty of the poor must be so hard for them. When looking for a home (for a centre) I walked and walked until my legs and arms ached. I thought how much they must ache in soul and body looking for a home, food and health. Then the comfort of Loreto came to tempt me, but of my own free choice, my God, and out of love for you, I desire to remain and do whatever be your holy will in my regard. Give me courage now, this moment."

Forsaking all worldly commitments and institutions, even refusing government aid, Mother Teresa has established a worldwide organization that ministers to the poor as they die. In 1979, when Mother Teresa won the Nobel Prize for Peace, she used the award money for her poor and dying people.

We live in a shrinking world that no longer allows us to believe we have nothing to do with a person halfway around the globe from us. We are all members of a "global community," and that makes everyone our neighbor. Our thoughts, our words, our actions will bless—or harm—all the people in the world.

For this reason we need to think very seriously about consuming the limited resources of our earth. In *The Predicament of the Prosperous,* Bruce C. Birch and Larry L. Rasmussen warn us that "there is no chance of the poor countries developing adequately unless the rich countries reduce the huge proportion they contribute to the total impact. The rich must live more simply that the poor may simply live."

Colman McCarthy, a Washington newspaperman, agrees when he writes: "In America, where overeating is so rampant that millions of citizens spend more money in weight-loss programs in a month than most people in the Third World earn in a year, it is enough merely to remember simply the standard and (conservative) figure: 500 million of the earth's poor are starving or severely malnourished."

Five hundred million people . . . I cannot ignore their silent pleas.

"But, Lord," I say, "what good can my little 'leftover' do?"

"I will swell the harvest of your benevolence," he replies, "and you will always be rich enough to be generous."

He knows what I need, and he knows he has given me more than that. I cannot refuse to reach out with bread in my hands.

## Chapter 14

## *The Bread of Compassion*

Mother Teresa says, "It matters not that you are called to serve the rich or the poor—it is the love you put into the doing." Love is the beginning and the end of sharing.

"I may dole out all I possess, or even give my body to be burnt, but if I have no love, I am none the better" (1 Cor. 13:3; NEB). In what is called the "love chapter," Paul tells us that love is not what we do, it's what we are. That is why love—and true sharing—are difficult. Love wants our sharing to do more than make us feel good, or simply relieved. Love wants to deal with real needs as effectively and sensitively as possible, and that may bring us suffering.

During a recent cold winter, an elderly woman in a large northeast city froze to death in her own apartment, without anyone knowing it. She couldn't afford to pay her heating bills, so the heat in her tiny apartment was turned off; the cold was so severe that the water pipes burst and water poured out all over the floor—and then froze. Days later, when the neighbors told the superintendent that "something wasn't right" in the old woman's apartment, the door was opened and the woman was found sitting in her chair, wrapped in blankets, dead.

"I don't understand how such a thing could have happened," the man who lived next door said. "She should have asked for help—she should have called out—anything." The officers of the utility company were horrified and explained that the heat shutoff was an automatic procedure in cases of nonpayment of bills. No one ever came around to investigate why the bills weren't paid—they didn't even know anything about the person who was supposed to pay them. It wasn't part of their responsibility.

To me, the saddest thing about this story is that there was no one close to this woman who cared enough to make her part of his or her responsibility. No one can take care of everyone—but everyone can take care of someone. God's love sets us free to care deeply about others, so when we are close to someone and see their need, we act. Doing things without love simply doesn't count, because acting out of a sense of spiritual "supremacy," moral indignation, or any other self-centered impulse makes us forget that we are poor, too.

Jesus, in his life on earth, was so aware of and so sensitive to human need that wherever he went people followed him, calling out to him, trying just to *touch* him. One woman touched the hem of his garment lightly—too shy to grab at his sleeve or shout to him for help—and he felt that touch. Immediately the woman's need was his concern, and he stopped to help her. A tax collector—a short, unobtrusive man—was full of self-loathing and remorse for the corruption of his life. Perhaps too ashamed to push through the crowd to Jesus, he climbed a tree to get a glimpse of him from a distance. But Jesus felt the man's need—felt it from a distance and through the crowd—and called to him to come down out of the tree so he could speak to him. And on that day the man began a new life because of Christ's ability to sense his need.

A prostitute, sensing that somehow he would understand her, was too choked with tears to tell Jesus how bitter her life was. All she could do was anoint his head with a very expensive oil and bathe his feet with her tears. But Jesus was sensitive to her need, and he restored her broken spirit with his affirming love and the forgiveness of her sins.

"But we *expect* it from him," we say. "After all, Jesus was God." Yes, and as his children—and disciples—we have been told to look after one another on his behalf, as though we were doing it unto him. Part of our responsibility as disciples is to grow in our capacity to sense the circumstances and needs of other people, and to learn to suffer with them. This is the meaning of compassion—to suffer along with someone.

". . . Jesus' teaching is never practical in the ordinary sense of the word, for it is based on an impractical commitment, a total trust in a new world order and its Ruler, for whom we must be prepared to suffer and die," writes Peter H. Davids in *Sojourner.* "Any radical commitment to him will result in a life-style of giving as well. . . . The command is unavoidable: Jesus loved and therefore gave. We are also to love and therefore give. The hand that remains closed in the face of need reveals a heart totally ignorant of Jesus, a life in which Jesus is anything but Lord."

In one of his early books, the late Dr. Frank Laubach, who was then a missionary to the people of the Philippines, described how he felt when he was caught up into the life of the Spirit, when his communion with God was so deep and rich that he felt his oneness with God. He said it made him feel wide open to God and his will, which was for him to begin a life of prayer. Then Dr. Laubach wrote: "And I added another resolve—to be as wide open to people and their need as I am towards God. Windows open outward as well as upward" (from *Letters by a Modern Mystic*).

Along the same line, Dr. Paul Rees, speaking about sensitivity, said: ". . . one of the values of prayer, if it be more than a verbal anesthetic, is that it gives the Spirit of God a chance to enliven our imagination, to sharpen our perception, and to deepen our emotion."

Love and sensitivity are the attitudes of sharing. But there is more. "Each person should give as he has decided for himself; there should be no reluctance, no sense of compulsion; God loves a cheerful giver" (2 Cor. 9:7; NEB). A "cheerful giver"—how lovely! It means that the life of sharing need not be a dreadful denial; it is joy and a clear sense of values and priorities. Although we should not give in order to receive joy, but rather to obey Christ, it is nevertheless true that in giving we do receive joy.

Think for a moment about your own family circle. Recall how happy you are when you can give your children, your life partner, your friends, or your parents something they want and cannot get for themselves. Remember that warm feeling flowing through you that made you offer up a silent prayer of thanks to God for giving you the opportunity to share something special with someone you love. There is joy in receiving —but it is nothing to compare with the joy of giving out of love.

"We must be able to radiate the joy of Christ, express it in our actions," says Mother Teresa. "If our actions are just useful actions that give no joy to the people, our poor people would never be able to rise up to the call which we want them to hear, the call to come closer to God. We want to make them feel that they are loved. If we went to them with a sad face, we would only make them much more depressed."

Whether love demands that we give to someone close or to someone far away, we can remember the words of Jesus that "anything we do for one of his brothers, however humble, we do for him." Even if we do not know the person we are called to help, Jesus does—and he wants to love his whole world through us.

"Jesus' . . . concern for the deliverance of the dispossessed was very concrete," write Bruce C. Birch and Larry L. Rasmussen in *The Predicament of the Prosperous*, "and his own life is witness to that concern. Jesus did associate himself with the poor, the captives, the blind, and the oppressed. Jesus healed and taught bringing wholeness and hope in a time of much suffering and despair. He befriended society's outcasts, tax collectors, prostitutes, lepers, lunatics, and poor people. For this he was greatly criticized by groups such as the Pharisees. 'Behold, a glutton and a drunkard, a friend of tax collectors and sinners' (Matthew 11:19)."

Back in the fifties, H. Richard Niebuhr was asking: "Who, finally, is my *neighbor?* . . . He is the near one and the far one, the one removed from me by distances in time and space, in convictions and loyalties. . . . The Neighbor is in past and present and future, yet he is not simply mankind in its totality but rather in its articulation, the community of individuals and individuals in community. He is Augustine in the Roman Catholic Church and Socrates in Athens, and the Russian people, and the unborn generations who will bear the consequences of our failures, future persons for whom we are administering the entrusted wealth of nature and other greater common gifts."

Anglican Bishop Festo Kivengere of Uganda, who withstood great persecution from his country's ousted ruler, Idi Amin, explains what is needed for our attitude of sharing as we share the bread of compassion: "You don't have to be extraordinary. Jesus seldom used extraordinary people. He takes them from the ordinary run of life, liberates them, forgives them, sets them free, and in wondering gratitude they put themselves at His disposal. Then what a change comes over them! Because He loved you so extravagantly, Jesus paid a tremendous price to make you the person you are. He held nothing back at all. God remained empty-handed when He gave you His beloved Son. Yet you remain, not empty-handed, but full when you give what you have to Jesus. Love Him with extravagance, and He will become the fulness of your life" (*Love Unlimited*).

It is out of this fullness that we have the bread of compassion to share. Author Gladys M. Hunt reminds us that "God holds us just as accountable for what we keep for ourselves as for what we give. Jesus still stands by the treasury.

"How much money would be available for a needy world if

all believers scaled down their standard of living, excites the imagination. How much glory would be given to the name of God, not only from the expansion of his Kingdom but from the purifying of it. What hinders believers from the carefree life-style Jesus talked about in his sermon when he said, 'Take no thought . . .'?"

# Chapter 15

## Dividing the Loaf

When we pray for our daily bread and our heavenly Father provides the loaf, we must remember that it is not ours alone. It must be divided—because there are those who do not know how to ask and those who do ask and whom God intends to answer through us. Some will receive their life resources only through our stewardship. Our daily bread then becomes the means to do what God wants us to do in this world. We have seen that Paul reminds us, "God can give you everything that you need, so that you may always have sufficient both for yourselves, and for giving away to other people" (2 Cor. 9:8; Phillips). So when our asking prayers get results—in whatever form—our work has just begun!

We can start with the giving of a tithe—which is far more than a gesture of support for one's church. We tithe to remind ourselves that all we are and have belongs to God, and that we are only stewards of his gifts and resources. In this day of emphasis on the self-made person, we need to be more aware of this dependency.

Some years ago the Church of the Savior of Washington, D.C., asked Reinhold Niebuhr to comment on the discipline of managing and tithing money, and I was very interested to read his response: "I would suggest that you commit yourselves not to tithing but to proportional giving, with tithing as an economic floor beneath which you will not go unless there are some compelling reasons." In the article containing this comment, author Elizabeth O'Connor explored Dr. Niebuhr's concept of *proportional giving* and found that it is proportionate not only to a family's wealth, but to a family's needs, a person's sense of security, and an awareness of those who suffer. It is *especially* proportionate to a person's sense of justice and of God's ownership of all things, even our *very lives.* Such giving proves that we are not simply "paying dues," but that we feel totally involved—materially, physically, spiritually, and emotionally—in God's Kingdom. It means we are loving and serving him with all our strength.

If the tithe is the floor beneath which we will not go, then whatever we give beyond the tithe becomes our offering to God, and the form and size of our offering will depend a great deal upon the way we choose to live. In other words, are we living according to our needs or our greeds?

"I found myself challenged to compassionate living," writes Arthur Maxwell Field, a resident of Koinonia, a Christian community near Americus, Georgia. "This is more than simple living, which is very 'in' now. Simple living can have many motives: I eat less so I will live longer or not get cancer; I reduce spending now so I can retire earlier; or go to Acapulco rather than south Georgia; I drive less out of patriotism.

"Compassionate living, as I see it, is a planned and expanding effort, in the name of Jesus Christ, to reduce my level of consumption for the sake of God's poor.

"It's not haphazard. I constantly learn of further steps I can take. It's a response to the fact that Jesus Christ is Lord. It makes funds and other resources available for the poor whom God loves so much, if we are to take the Bible seriously" (*As I See It Today,* Union Seminary, Richmond, Va., April 1979).

I like the term "compassionate living." To me, it means living with others in our hearts—making our choices with the consideration of their needs in mind. For many of us, learning to live compassionately will include steps toward a simpler life-style. At least, that is what it means for me and my family —but not in a way that makes simplicity an end in itself. Thomas Merton gives us a clue to our proper motivation by saying, "We do not detach ourselves from things in order to attach ourselves to God, but rather we become detached from ourselves in order to see and use all things in and for God" (*Thomas Merton on Prayer*). We simplify, not to make things easier for ourselves—although that is often a welcome fringe benefit—but to make things better for others.

We need to step back and take a look at what we have, and then at what we need. With that kind of self-detachment, we can make "a planned and expanding effort, in the name of Jesus Christ, to reduce [our] level of consumption for the sake of God's poor."

But reducing consumption may not be enough. Anytime we can emphasize the quality of life and relationships rather than the quantity of material things accumulated, we will be taking steps in the right direction. And we can do this in so many practical ways: by conserving some of the materials we use, such as fuel and other forms of energy, paper goods and disposable products; by recycling organic garbage in our gardens; and by simplifying our eating habits—which takes some real skill and planning! Becoming aware of our own values may be one of the most important things we can ever do for our children—and if we can articulate them and reevaluate them with our children, we will be opening new channels of vital communication between them and us.

"Many wealthy children go through a stage of questioning," said Dr. Robert Coles, a psychiatrist. "They hear words at Church that cause them to think of justice and injustice. In their innocence, they ask what Christ would be like if he came back. Would he identify with the rich or with the poor and humble? When they ask such questions, they get a little nervous. I wish their parents would experience the same nervousness. But when they are confronted with the central message of the Bible, they don't. Rather, they teach their children not to ask why the world is the way it is. After a while the children forget their ethical questions about life. It's far easier for them just to go along" (*The Other Side,* May 1979).

In our family—as in many others I know—our four children were the ones who first awakened us to many ways we could simplify our lives. Less bound by tradition, their living habits not deeply entrenched, they were extremely receptive to sensible, practical ways in which we could cut down our consumption of endangered natural resources. Whenever possible, walking and, especially, biking were fine with them, and public transportation was fast and inexpensive. Clothes? Well, a few nice things, but jeans were acceptable for most occasions. Nutrition came first as far as food was concerned, and when it came to the use of energy, they adjusted our thermostat—literally and figuratively—in many areas of our family life. Yes, our kids led the way at our house, and Louie and I, seeing the results, were happy to follow with enthusiasm.

At the moment, my husband and I still need two cars because often we have to go in different directions and to places where public transportation cannot take us. But our cars serve us long and well (would you believe?—240,000 miles on our last car!), thanks to the fact that we have a few excellent mechanics in our family who keep them in good running condition year after year.

Recently we made an important decision about our house, which we liked very much, but which was larger than we needed now that our children are older and away at school. We sold the house and moved into a much smaller house in the city, where we will soon be able to eliminate one of our cars in favor of public transportation in the form of Washington's new Metro system. The new "old" house, being smaller and attached to another, will consume less engery for heating; its tiny backyard will also save our human energy when it comes to keeping the grass mowed. Louie likes that!

These are some of the ways that are working for us as a

family. But they will not work for everyone, and this is a point I hasten to make.

Simplification is important in our lives today, but not everyone will be able to simplify in the same ways. What is possible, and even pleasurable, for one person—or one family—may not be possible or wise for another.

Over a recent Christmas holiday, when our family had the rare experience of being all together at the same time, we and our children took a short retreat at a beach in South Carolina. It was a lovely, quiet time, and one night we treated ourselves by going out to eat in a restaurant. And, of course, sitting there, waiting for our food, we began to talk about food, specifically the lack of it in so many parts of the world. Then one of our children said, "Do you realize that this meal is going to cost us almost as much as we give to the Hunger Committee every month?"

Well, I think we all felt somewhat guilty about that, and I, especially, began to be uncomfortable . . . because if there is anything I really enjoy, it's eating out. It refreshes me—and I do cook a lot of meals at home and for groups, so it's nice to have a change. "I don't think I'd like to give up an occasional dinner out," I confessed.

And as we went around the table, each one of us found that there were a few things in our lives that would be tough for us to eliminate. One son enjoys traveling with his backpack and sleeping bag. He glows with the stimulation of seeing new places and meeting new people; to him it is not only recreational, but educational. Louie is in a partnership with a group of men who fly, and he loves to fly that plane, not just as a way to get to speaking engagements, but as a much-needed form of relaxation. And there were other things each of us realized it would be a struggle for us to give up. Not that we wouldn't if we had to . . . but did everyone have to give up the same things, or live in exactly the same way? Some people would say yes, yet I don't think God requires us to conform to one mold. I think it is more important for us to find ways in which each of us *can* simplify—needless to say, that conversation around the table made all of us realize we had only just begun.

We must be aware that in our attempt to live responsibly we do not become judgmental in our attitude toward others in their attempts to do the same thing, but in different ways. And so, while I enjoy living in the city, near the subway, I realize it is not the life-style for everyone. There is still a need for suburbs, and for the country. . . . Some of us may not need a car at all, while others may really need more than one. The important thing is to acknowledge all we have and are as belonging to God—and to be his willing and joyful stewards in the world.

Peter H. Davids believes that "no Christian should rest comfortably with his life-style so long as it allows him to live with a surplus while a brother or sister somewhere in the world is suffering relievable want.

"The Christian life-style is a simple life-style, for it gives instead of hoards and limits instead of consumes. . . . The greatness and the severity of the demand is matched only by the power of the One who calls us to it."

Frank E. Gaebelein writes: ". . . our creation in God's image . . . compels us to see whether anything in the way we live tends to diminish or degrade our humanity. . . . The Biblical principle of the relationship of humanity to God's world is not ownership but stewardship.

". . . The Old Testament refers many times, and not always negatively, to prosperity and riches. Yet it also insistently warns against the idolatry of material things and allowing them to turn our hearts from God . . . the progressive aggrandizement that leads people into life-styles in which almost everything is spent on self and only a pittance is given to help the poor and hungry.

". . . We must not tolerate anything in our life-style that will diminish our brother or sister for whom Christ died."

In determining how much we should simplify, Dr. Gaebelein suggests that we apply these "hard questions" to our life-style: "Does an indulgent life-style betray a failure in love? Is increasing expenditure on material things depriving our poor and hungry neighbors of help? Is idolatry of things impairing the integrity of our love for God?" Hard, yes . . . but also necessary—and right.

While compassionate living starts with the individual and the family, there are many things we can do as groups, especially within the church. One attempt to encourage the congregation we serve to focus on life-styles began in 1975 when a small band of concerned people felt led to do something, however small, about alleviating world hunger. But what to do? A special collection? A fair? A rummage sale? All of these time-honored but tired methods seemed to miss the point. It was all too easy for many of us in our relatively well-to-do congregation simply to write another check. What we needed was something to make us examine our own lives and discover the meaning of sacrificial giving.

After studying hunger and learning what other interested groups were doing, we decided to develop a Hunger Covenant. People were urged to covenant with the Lord to sacrifice something that would simplify their life-style or eliminate a wasteful practice in order to accumulate funds for a Hunger Committee. To dramatize the need, we invited the congregation to a dinner—but not any ordinary dinner. Chosen at random, some people were served a delicious chicken dinner, some a low-cost meal, and some only a single boiled potato. And it worked. It enabled all of us to come to grips with our emotions—resentment, self-pity, embarrassment, guilt—as some of us ate lavishly and others looked on hungrily.

The dinner was a huge success, although only a small percentage of the congregation actually made the covenant—but enough to get something done and encourage the effort. Each year the giving grows slowly and steadily, with bursts of generosity toward specific needy areas. Recently one Sunday's gifts for the hungry in a devastated foreign country amounted to as much as we used to receive in an entire year.

The things people have chosen to give up often reflect their middle-class culture. For example, some saw it not only as an opportunity for generosity, but as an encouragement to discipline themselves in a battle against smoking. Some began carrying lunch bags to work instead of eating expensive, often excessive restaurant fare. Others served a meatless dinner once a week, or gave up fertilizer for the lawn, while one couple decided to eliminate grain alcohol at their frequent dinner parties. One of my friends, Frances, saves all her supermarket sales slips and gives a percentage tithe to the Hunger Committee, and a young man who lives in Bethesda and works on Capitol Hill rides his bike approximately twenty-five miles back and forth each day if weather permits to save gas and money. In church, tables have been set aside for weekly donations of food, some of it going to the hungry in the District of Columbia, and some to needy church members.

Radically changed lives? No. But, we hope, consciousness raising . . . increased sensitivity . . . a first step.

Our next efforts were directed toward developing an Urban Ministry Team. Half of our Hunger Funds went to the poor in Washington, but since many of us had never set foot in a truly depressed area, it was suggested that some people donate time and talent to serve the needy, and perhaps in the process develop greater understanding. In cooperation with minority leaders involved in similar ministries, and specifically with One Ministries led by John Staggers, interested people in the congregation began to go into one specific block of Washington, D.C. to clean, paint, and repair rundown buildings, and one day recently ended with the arrival of other congregation members bearing the makings of a pot-luck dinner. As workers and residents of the area gathered in the basement of a local church for fellowship together with song and laughter, you could hear a guitar solo, then a chorus of "Amazing Grace." A wizened old lady sang her own song to a soul beat. An elderly blind man gave his all to "What a Friend We Have in Jesus." It was a joyous, spontaneous, loving experience—an opportunity to build relationships. Urban Task Force workers go home from these experiences with a new sense of commitment and a hundred questions. What good does it do simply to paint and clean up? How can we do more than apply Band-Aids? How can we help to overcome the depression—and oppression—that gets in the way of people helping themselves? What are the roots of poverty and powerlessness? Are these root problems a spiritual matter? For them? For us?

And then a small group of us became involved in another small effort: a seminar series devoted to grappling with these very questions and many more, entitled "The Wrestlers: Where the Rubber Meets the Road." A group of us meets every Sunday between services to discuss the real meaning of Christian commitment in our lives. We have had guests from the Sojourners or the Church of the Savior and other groups come to share their way of living out commitment, of simplifying lifestyles, of dealing with social problems within a Christian context. Out of this we hope will come greater life-style changes, greater commitment to action—a deep, honest look at a Christian and *money*. Some are already paving the way. A middle-aged couple with grown children move from an expensive suburban neighborhood to a modest city apartment to be closer to their areas of Christian mission. A couple in similar circumstances buy an apartment house on Capitol Hill and become intensely involved in the problems of the poor in that area. Several families moving into the same inner-city block form a "community of ministry." Many others are honestly looking for ways to live and model Christian love in the community.

There are other creative ways to share resources. A group of young married couples in our church found a way to work together—supporting one another at the same time that they simplify their housing repair costs. They all had small children and only one income. The husbands worked very hard and, like most men starting out, put in long hours on the job. They had hardly any time for the things that needed to be done around the home, and no money to employ someone else to do it. As they became frustrated by roofs that leaked when it rained, plumbing that dripped through the night, attics that ushered cold air into the rest of the house, and countless other broken things that needed fixing over a long period of time, tempers became short and accusations of neglect were made.

One reason these couples were drawn together was their ability to empathize with one another's feelings. Then, as they began to meet together to study and share, they also began to pray for one another's needs. And suddenly an answer came in the form of a very bright idea. Since none of the couples had enough time to repair their own home, why not pool their time and work together on each home—one at a time? They tried it, and it worked! Once a month, on a Saturday, all the couples meet at one house and do whatever needs doing. The children play together, the parents work all day at the tasks, and in the evening they share a pot-luck "agape" supper. Everyone has a great time. It takes a long time to get around to each house, but the couples can put up with the waiting because they know the work will get done now. To me this is a beautiful, practical example of God energizing people through their sensitivity to one another's needs—a great idea!

Yes, the loaf must be divided—and into many pieces, for there are many needs. And the One who hears us praying for our daily bread will give us more creative ideas as we become more willing to share. We can also learn from one another.

As I hope I have made very clear, I am only a beginner in this pilgrimage toward compassionate living, and I have found it helpful to know what others are doing to achieve this life-style. One of the richest sources of information comes to me from newsletters circulated by such organizations as Bread for the World, working in the area of hunger; Habitat for Humanity, in the area of housing for the poor; and Evangelicals for Social Action, in the area of overall social justice; World Vision; and the little magazine *The Other Side*—and there are many others. Surely some of them have reached out to you. You will find in their example and in their literature a wealth of creative opportunities to share your life resources with those who need them, and so become a responsible steward for God.

More specifically, there are several practical steps each of us can take in linking our lives with those of others with whom we are interdependent:

We can give regularly to our church's relief agency. I know how often you must have heard such appeals from your denomination, as I have, but have you ever realized what a "good deal" the offer is? Unlike many other charitable organizations, the church relief agency has a very low overhead, so that the proportion of money and services delivered to those in need is very high and all that is given is in the name of Christ. It deserves your support and mine.

Each of us can become a citizen advocate of a sharing lifestyle by communicating our concerns about world hunger and conservation, and other issues that haunt us, to our congressional representatives. While it is true that we cannot legislate hunger out of our world, we can affect the way the world's food is distributed—and that is a beginning! For instance, in 1979 a bill was introduced into Congress by Senator Mark Hatfield and several others, encouraging a tax credit of 10 percent for farmers who gave surplus, unharvested, damaged, or otherwise wasted food commodities to various nonprofit, charitable organizations for distribution to the poor and needy. It was known as "The Gleaner's Bill," after the Old Testament custom of allowing the poor to glean what was left from the harvest of a farmer's fields. As the bill explained, "based on the average daily caloric intake of a U.S. citizen, . . . the grains, meat, sugar, oilseeds, vegetables, fruits, and nuts in 1974 could have fed an estimated 49 million people." We need to be informed about this kind of legislation so we can give it our support.

We can become well informed about the needs of our world by reading—newspapers, newsletters, books, and by listening to those who know and care.

We can share our concern and our information with our friends and enlist their support of relief projects. If there isn't a Hunger Committee in your church, you can start one!

We can talk about our life-style and our values with our family members, and, we hope, grow away from an emphasis on the material and toward the compassionate. We can focus on quality rather than quantity.

We can pray—for *our* daily bread (with special emphasis on the *our*) . . . for an awareness of need throughout the world . . . for a Christlike response to those needs . . . for those who are trying to alleviate hunger and pain and misery . . . and for those who cry out to us for help.

Compassionate living is a blessing that awaits us. "Give us this day our daily bread" is more than a request, even more than a plea in times of distress or urgency. It is a relationship of a child to a loving Father. It is a practical, day-by-day expression of our Christian faith, a bond between God, ourselves, and others. And for these reasons it is important for us to know not only how and when to speak these words, but how to build our lives around them—through asking . . . through receiving our bread from God . . . and, as his joyful stewards, through dividing the loaf he gives with the world he loves.

EPILOGUE


That farmer handing round the bread had made no gift to us at table: he had shared with us and exchanged with us that bread in which all of us had our part. And by that sharing the farmer had not been impoverished but enriched. He had eaten sweeter bread, bread of the community, by that sharing.

Antoine de Saint-Exupéry, *Flight to Arras*